Sketches of a Small Town…circa 1940… a memoir

CLIFTON K. MEADOR M.D.

ISBN-10: 149917439X
ISBN-13: 9781499174397
Library of Congress Control Number: 2014907362
CreateSpace Independent Publishing Platform
North Charleston, South Carolina

"Whenever I'm asked why Southern writers particularly have a penchant for writing about freaks, I say it is because we are still able to recognize one."

— Flannery O'Connor
In Southern Writers

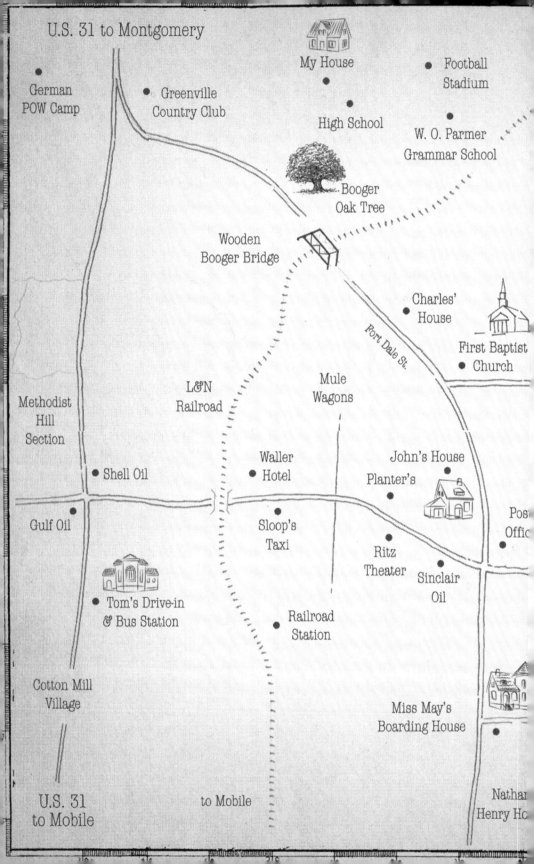

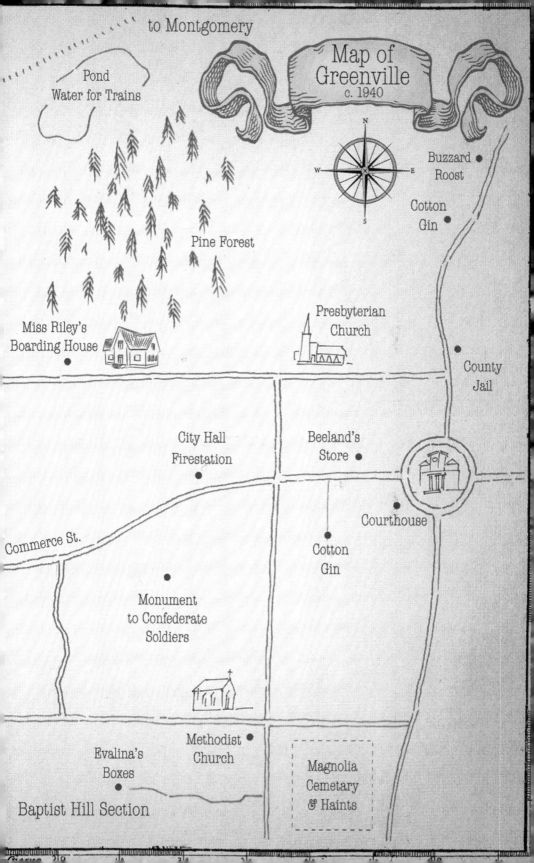

Other books by
Clifton K. Meador, M.D.

1. Meador, C.K., A_Little Book of Doctors' Rules, Hanley & Belfus, Inc., November, 1992.
2. Lanius, R.H., Meador, C.K., A Little Book of Nurse's Rules, Hanley & Belfus, Inc., 1993.
3. Wadlington, W. and Meador, C.K., Pearls from a Pediatric Practice, Hanley & Belfus, Inc.,1998.
4. Meador, C.K., A Little Book of Doctors' Rules II, A Compilation, Hanley & Belfus, Inc., 1999.
5. Slovis, C.M., Wrenn, K.D., Meador, C.K., A Little Book of Emergency Medicine Rules, Hanley & Belfus, Inc., 2000.
6. Wadlington, W., Meador, C.K., Howington, M. How to Raise Healthy and Happy Children, iUniverse, Inc., 2001
7. Meador, C.K., Med School, Hillsboro Press, Providence Publishing Corporation, 2003
8. Meador, C.K., Symptoms of Unknown Origin, A Medical Odyssey, Vanderbilt University Press, 2005.
9. Meador, C.K., Twentieth Century Men in Medicine: Personal Reflections, iUniverse, Inc., 2007
10. Meador, C.K., Puzzling Symptoms: how to solve the puzzle of your symptoms, Cable Publishing, Brule, WI, 2008
11. Meador, C.K., Med School, Revised Edition. Cable Publishing, Brule, WI, 2009.
12. Meador, C.K., True Medical Detective Stories. CreateSpace, North Charleston, SC. 2012.
13. Meador, C.K., Fascinomas– fascinating medical mysteries. CreateSpace, North Charleston, SC. 2013.

Acknowledgments

In the 20 years that I have been writing these stories, many people have read drafts or listened to readings. I am indebted to all of them for criticisms and suggestions. In 1995, I read an early draft to the "Old Oaks Club" my local reading and writing club, celebrating its 125th year. The comments from that evening encouraged me to add more stories.

More recently, my other writing club (The Scribblers) reviewed some of the chapters, giving many helpful ideas and suggestions for improvements. Members of the club are Barry Jones, Alan Graber, Frank Freemon, Ann Walsh, Anne Lane, Robin Andrews, and Lee Koehn.

Other readers include my daughters Ann Meador Shayne, Elizabeth Meador Driskill, and Mary Kathleen Meador. Harold and Charles Chambliss, brothers, made extremely helpful suggestions. Both grew up in Greenville. Charles features prominently in the stories and remains my oldest and best friend. Others who have read and made suggestions include Caroline Russell, Francis Beeland Givhan, Alice Meador, Oscar and Jane Crofford, John Norris, Sarah Fleming, Steve Condurelis, Graham Meador (my son), and Dr. William Mundy.

Beth Stein, my editor guided me every step and transformed the stories into a book. I cannot thank her enough for all she did to improve the writings. Whatever faults remain are my doings, not hers.

I appreciate the artistic work and talent of Mark Cowden for his cover design and for producing the map of Greenville. Mark has won several prestigious National Addy awards for his graphic designs.

Finally, there is my wife Ann Cowden Meador, a portrait artist in her own right and mother of Mark Cowden. She read each word and chapter as I drafted them, finding many errors and omissions. The book is a very different book from all of her careful and detailed readings.

I hope all of my children, grandchildren, and great granddaughter will enjoy these stories of my growing up in a different time and place, gone forever.

Table of Contents

Acknowledgements · ix
Prologue;   The Cemetery: January, 2001 · · · · · · · · · · · xiii
Chapter 1   The Town · 1
Chapter 2   Fried Methodist Chicken and
             The First Baptist Church · · · · · · · · · · · · · · 7
Chapter 3   Frisky · 13
Chapter 4   Billy · 17
Chapter 5   John · 21
Chapter 6   Charles · 27
Chapter 7   World War II · · · · · · · · · · · · · · · · · 31
Chapter 8   Leon and Pearl · · · · · · · · · · · · · · · · 37
Chapter 9   Frog · 41
Chapter 10   Mister Billy's Morning Glories · · · · · · · · · 49
Chapter 11   Mister Gus · · · · · · · · · · · · · · · · · · 53
Chapter 12   The Trains · · · · · · · · · · · · · · · · · · 61
Chapter 13   Professor Orville G. Harding · · · · · · · · · · 67
Chapter 14   Miss B and Miss Caroline · · · · · · · · · · · 73
Chapter 15   Mamie and Boogers · · · · · · · · · · · · · · 79
Chapter 16   The Reverend Ralph Morgan · · · · · · · · · · 85
Chapter 17   Sloop · 93
Chapter 18   Quail Hunting with My Father · · · · · · · · · 97
Chapter 19   Ruby · 105
Chapter 20   Buzzard Hunting · · · · · · · · · · · · · · · · 111
Chapter 21   John Charles Roberts · · · · · · · · · · · · · · 115
Chapter 22   Mister Lum and Louise · · · · · · · · · · · · · 123
Chapter 23   Miss Irene and Mister Hudson · · · · · · · · · 129
Chapter 24   Wildcats and Country Boys · · · · · · · · · · · 135

Clifton K. Meador M.D.

Chapter 25 Grady and Lucy · 139
Chapter 26 Rabbit Hunting with Tootsie · · · · · · · · · · · · 143
Chapter 27 Roosevelt Tells All · · · · · · · · · · · · · · · · · · · 147
Chapter 28 The 1947 Greenville High School
           Basketball Team · · · · · · · · · · · · · · · · · · · 153
Chapter 29 Mrs. Nathan Henry · · · · · · · · · · · · · · · · · · 157
Chapter 30 The Final Curtain: The Blue and Grey Parade · · 161
Epilogue   May 1, 2014 · 167
About the Author · 171

Prologue

The Cemetery

January, 2001

I am standing at the graveside funeral of one of my oldest friends, John Sherling, who died in his sleep two days ago. We first met in kindergarten in 1936, when we were 5 years old. "Big John" is what the preacher calls him. Everybody in the town called him by that name.

I see Charles Chambliss off to my right. He came up from Mobile, 150 miles to the south. Charles and John are my closest and oldest friends. Charles and I will visit after the funeral. He nods as I catch his attention.

The preacher is telling stories about Big John. How he set the speed record to Montgomery in an Olds '88 in 1947. "Even now that record still stands," he says. I smile. I was the one who held the stopwatch as co-pilot on that memorable trip. John ran from the Greenville Country Club to the Southern Dairy Plant just south of Montgomery -- around 40 miles -- in exactly 31 minutes and 20 seconds. I remember it like it was yesterday.

Clifton K. Meador M.D.

The preacher continues with more of John's fast driving stories. The time John got his car tangled in deep kudzu and another time when he hit a mule, knocking the mule almost 50 yards without killing it. "And Big John was fast in life just as he was in driving a car," the preacher continues. The crowd assembled by John's grave laughs, some shaking their heads in feigned disbelief. John was notorious for dating a lot of different women. The preacher mentions this as a sign of John's "loving disposition," actually winking as he says it.

As he goes on about John, I begin to remember more and more stories of my own. I begin to chuckle quietly, recalling the time John, Charles and I got in trouble setting a field on fire. And the other times we hid from Mister Gus, the chief of police.

I drove down from Nashville last night to be here, and although I drove by myself, I was never really alone. Hundreds of memories and images whirled through my mind. I have not been in Greenville in many years. Early this morning, I drove through the streets of the town alone remembering that at one time I knew who lived in every house, who they married and where they worked (if they worked at all). And they all knew me. And whenever we saw each other we always spoke or just waved. Everyone in those days spoke or waved or both.

Greenville was a special place for me. Momma and Daddy had picked it out as a small town to raise two boys – my older brother Dan and me. In the early '30s at the bottom of the Great Depression, Daddy was lucky to get a traveling job with the L&N Railroad. We had to move from Selma so Daddy would be on the main line. The L&N ran from Louisville through Nashville all the way through Alabama down to New Orleans. Momma and Daddy traveled up and down that line through Tennessee, Alabama and Mississippi looking for the ideal small town. They chose Greenville, Alabama.

The Cemetery January, 2001

Driving around the town this morning, I realized that most of those who were near and dear to me have died or moved away. Those who are still alive, I can barely recognize. Even so, familiar sights transported me back to my childhood here. The people and stories of my youth surfaced in my mind and surrounded me once more. This is the place I grew up, went to Miss Frances Cater's Kindergarten, nearly died with pneumonia, attended W.O. Parmer Grammar School, broke my arm, played basketball and trombone, finished high school and chased a girl who broke my heart. I was raised here, formed my values and beliefs here, and eventually became the person I am. After my mother died when I was 13, the whole town, like a village, raised me. After my father's death in 1965, I rarely returned except for short visits to see my stepmother. I had lost track of the town and nearly all of the people here. Until now.

As I passed each house and turned each corner of the town, the memories of childhood and teenage flooded into my thoughts. Particular moments from my past replayed over and over in my mind. I began to remember the hilarious stories, full of remarkable characters – Greenville's lone cross-dressing transsexual, Frog the beloved retarded adult, Roosevelt who knew all about women, and Pearl, classmate and daughter of the town whore. And then there was Leon, a clever country boy with a gift for elaborate pranks. This town may have been small, but my life growing up here among all these people was anything but dull.

Someone once asked Flannery O'Connor why Southern writers write about kooky people. She replied that the South was the only region in the country that could still tell them from more normal people. It never occurred to me that the people who surrounded me in Greenville all those years ago were anything but normal. Now, looking back on all of it, I realized what a treasure of characters and stories I have packed away in memory. I knew they were worth sharing.

Clifton K. Meador M.D.

Of course, memories are mere glimpses of our past; they are incomplete. Disconnected, they jump into our minds and then fade away. Throughout this book are sketches of the characters that made up the life of the town as I remember them. In the background are the mid-century forces that shaped all of us: religion, social class, race, sex, voodoo and other superstitions and a Second World War that engulfed the town and the nation.

The stories that follow are brief moments of my life. I have altered a few of the names where I thought appropriate to protect feelings and longstanding ties. These are some of my fondest memories from childhood to puberty to adolescence into early adulthood in the small town of Greenville, Alabama, in the South in the 1930s and '40s.

One

THE TOWN

There are several numerical ways to size a small town. Some people use traffic lights. We called them "red lights." There were three in Greenville: one at the top of the hill by the Gulf and Shell stations, one at mid Commerce Street across from the post office and the Sinclair Station, and one at the railroad overpass just in front of the three-story wooden Waller Hotel, Greenville's only hotel. That's where the traveling salesmen sat in rocking chairs on the sidewalk.

There was only one taxi. There were two barbershops and one picture show, the Ritz Theater. There were two piano teachers, my friend Charles reminded me. His mother was one of them.

These days, small towns are sized by the number of tanning spas or Dairy Queens. Tanning spas didn't exist in my day, of course, but neither did Dairy Queen. If Dairy Queens had existed, I would put Greenville at about a one-and-a-half Dairy Queen town.

Of all the ways of sizing a small town by numbers, however, I think I've come up with a novel one. I don't know how to say this any other way but to say it: Greenville was a two-whore town.

Louise was on the north side of town and Maw Gooden to the south. Louise's daughter Pearl was my classmate for nine years, until she dropped out of school in the ninth grade. More on that later.

As to the economy, Greenville was a cotton town. Its seasons were cotton seasons. In spring, there were the aromas of fertilizer, of seeds, of the metallic smells of plows and new rope and the peculiar odor of newly plowed dirt mixed with leather, and the distinctive odors of laboring black men. In summer, it was the faint odors of the sap of growing things and roots and sweat and dirt -- always dirt. July's noxious air reeked of boll weevil poisons, but the late heat of August and early fall welcomed the unmistakable aroma of picked cotton. In ginning time, sometimes the lint was so thick in the air you could see it in the sunlit doorways of the stores. And then there were the delicious, almost edible aromas of cottonseeds. At cotton-picking time, if the weather was dry, which a cotton farmer hoped for, there was a red clay dustiness to everyone and everything that came into town. The streets were lined with high-topped mule-drawn wagons brimming with cotton waiting to be ginned. In winter, all this activity ceased. Farming stopped except for killing hogs. The winter people smelled of wood fires and smoke mixed with the salty scents of cooked ham.

Everything was built around cotton. Greenville had two cotton gins owned by separate families who also operated the two all-purpose general stores. Everything for farmers was purchased by what was called "on account" -- the saying was "on account of I don't have any money." Clothes, food, seed, fertilizer, rope lines, plows, mules, wagons -- whatever the family needed was "purchased" and recorded in the little book each owner of the store and gin carried in his hip pocket. After cotton picking time, after the ginning and, most important, after the price of cotton was determined, these accounts were settled. As a result of this credit/trade arrangement, most farmers took away little or no cash. But if cotton prices

The Town

were up, they had all the goods they needed. If cotton prices were low, well, it was a long cold winter. Merle Haggard sings of it in his song *If We Make It Through December.*

When I was in the sixth grade, I began working Saturdays at one of these general stores, Planter's Mercantile. It was owned by the Haygood family who also owned one of the two gins. Farmers frequently came in and mistakenly asked for "Mister Planters." I always took them to the owner, the elder Mister Jim Haygood. Mister Jim carried the little black book in his back pocket. He was the only person with the authority to give credit. I never saw him smile.

Two black men, Tootsie and his assistant Roosevelt, ran the backend of the store. Having just turned 11 in 1942, I was put to work as an assistant clerk under both men. We sold all the equipment needed for mule farming, plus staples such as flour, sugar, beans, fatback pork, cheese and a few canned goods, plus sugar cane molasses. After Mister Jim nodded that he had given credit, the farmers would pull their mule-drawn wagons to the side door where Roosevelt and I loaded the purchases. Tootsie, who was in charge, supervised us. You will get to know Tootsie and Roosevelt later.

The other general store was Beeland's, owned by the Beeland family. The Beelands and the Haygoods sat at the top of Greenville's socio- economic heap. Next in these sophisticated strata were the Ford and Chevrolet dealers, followed by the three men who owned the Shell, Sinclair or Gulf gasoline/oil distributors, which the farmers pronounced "dis'- try -bew'-turs." After the oil distributors came the combination undertaker/hardware store owner, then the furniture store owner and then all the lesser shop owners. I forgot the probate judge and the postmaster who were just under the car dealers. There were three lawyers and three doctors, who were somewhere between the gin owners and the car dealers. One of

Clifton K. Meador M.D.

the doctors was a distant cousin of my good friend John. One of the lawyers was drunk most of the time and depended on his wife who taught high school English. Actually the lawyer was not only drunk, he was also one of the town's invalids, allegedly having been gassed in World War I -- a story no one really believed, but no one dared confront either. The wife was from a good enough family that the lawyer was still accepted, albeit with some skepticism.

Back to numbers, as mentioned there were three brands of gasoline sold at three filling stations. Mister Billy ran the Sinclair station by the Ritz Theater downtown and across from the post office. Mister Lane Grass, who ran the Gulf station up on the hill by the water tower and across from Tom's Drive-in and Bus Station. Mister Dan, father of my best friend John, ran the Shell station across the street from the Gulf station. In addition to the three service stations, there were three civic clubs: Rotary, Lions and Kiwanis.

As was typically the case in Southern small towns those days, religion was a dominant part of life in Greenville. There were three main churches, not counting several small edge-of-town Pentecostal types known as "Holy Rollers." These three were Methodist, Baptist and Presbyterian. There was a small Episcopal congregation that only had services once a month, so most of the Episcopalians split the rest of the time between the Methodist and Presbyterian churches. There were only 13 Catholics, one Jew, whose wife and daughter continued to live in New York, and three Republicans. There were no Yankees until Frankie moved to town in the second grade. More on Frankie later.

Thus, there were three men's clubs, three religious affiliations and three brands of gasoline in town. The combinations of club, religion and gasoline were socially defining. There was no crossing over. For example, you could be Kiwanis, Presbyterian and Shell or you might be Lions, Methodist and Sinclair or even Baptist,

The Town

Rotary and Gulf. Any combination was acceptable; you just had to stick with it. Changing filling station affiliations was as big a deal as changing religions or maybe even sexual preference. I know this firsthand. My father started out Rotarian, Baptist and Gulf. In later years, he switched from Gulf to Shell, thus becoming Rotarian, Baptist and Shell. He never got over how much he hurt Mister Lane who owned the Gulf station at the top of the hill, across from Mister Dan's Shell station.

Beyond the rather comical allegiances to civic clubs and gasolines, there were more serious divisions in this South Alabama town. Not surprisingly, Greenville in those days was sharply divided into two unbridgeable sections – white and black.

There were two black sections of town, immediately adjacent to the white sections. Baptist Hill lay to the south of town and Methodist Hill to the west. The boundary for each was clearly marked by where the asphalt paving stopped and the street turned to red clay. In the rainy season, those clay streets became impassable.

This was the time of complete and rigid separation of the races – so called "separate but equal." Integration was more than 20 years in the future. Separation of the races was the culture taught to every white child at an early age and drilled into every black child as a fact of life. This ugly separation permeated everything, and everything was marked. Water fountains read "White" and "Colored," as did all the separate waiting rooms at the two hospitals, law offices, courts at the courthouse, waiting rooms at the train station and the few public toilets. All buses required blacks to sit at the back. All restaurants were for "Whites Only," as was the Waller Hotel. The Ritz Theater let whites sit on the main floor, but blacks had to sit in the balcony accessed through a separate set of outside steps. Whites and blacks attended separate schools. For whites, intermingling with blacks socially was as taboo as incest. In those days, no one dared breach this separation, as I would find out at a very early age.

Clifton K. Meador M.D.

The prejudices in Greenville were not limited to blacks versus whites. The white section also had its own class system. The largest social and economic division was between those in Cotton Mill Village and the rest of the town. It was in some ways as confining as the black/white boundaries, even though all whites attended the same schools. There was no social mingling between these two white cultures, however, as separated as by the Berlin Wall. Beyond this group, there were also whites defined as "country" or "city" depending on where they grew up. Anybody who rode the school bus was labeled a "country boy." There were tensions here, too. More on that later.

Life in Greenville was very quiet and private. People went to work, attended church on Sunday and listened to the nightly radio programs. The small country club was not a center of social life but served only as a nine hole golf course. Neighbors knew each other but rarely entertained. The men's business clubs were the main sources of social contact. Almost all the wives stayed home, totally devoted to being mothers.

This was the town of Greenville when my family moved there on September 7, 1936, my fifth birthday.

Two

Fried Methodist Chicken and

The First Baptist Church

R eligious affiliation in Greenville, like so many other things, imposed yet another subtle-yet-defining social ranking. Episcopalians were on top, then Presbyterians, then Methodists, then Baptists, followed by Pentecostals and a host of small churches on the edge of town and out in the country.

Ranking had nothing to do with the size of the churches. In fact, it seemed almost inverse to size of the congregations; there were more Baptists in Greenville than any other religion. I never questioned these social rankings. Looking back, they seemed to correlate with members' incomes and the size of their houses and the makes of their cars. It reminds me of an old joke about how the religions settled the Wild West. They say Baptist preachers went west on horseback; Presbyterian preachers went later by stage-coach; and Episcopalian ministers went last. The Episcopalians were waiting until they could go by train in nice Pullman cars.

Someone also told me that Methodists were just Baptists who could read. I'm glad Momma never heard that. Momma was raised

7

by a stern and strict Scot Presbyterian, but she switched to Baptist when she married Daddy. She would have been offended that anyone thought poorly of her adopted church. Even though Momma was outwardly a Baptist, she remained a Presbyterian at heart. As a child, I lived under the Grace of the God of the First Baptist Church overseen by Momma and her Presbyterian God. It was a lot.

Being raised part Baptist and part Presbyterian by my mother had its own rigidity. If Momma had been a man, she would have been a preacher. She was completely devout and determined that her sons would live under the grace of God. She saw that we never missed a service at the First Baptist Church, starting with Sunday School, then morning worship, then Baptist Training Union (BTU) at night, followed by the Sunday night service in the church. Every Wednesday night we went to prayer service.

In addition, I was a member of the Royal Ambassadors or "RAs" as we called it. Royal Ambassadors was a Baptist club for preteen boys. We met weekly and did projects to help the poor, like collecting can goods and used clothing. We always marched into church carrying the flag and singing *Onward Christian Soldiers*. In the summer we went to a special Royal Ambassador weekend camp north of Montgomery. My early youth was completely immersed in the Baptist Church under the constant supervision of Momma.

Beyond monitoring the religious life of my brother Dan and me, she was also heavily involved herself. When the visiting evangelist came to town each summer to lead the annual revival, Momma invited him home for dinner. She served as head of the Women's Mission Union (WMU) that met regularly every week. Besides a gathering for Bible reading, the WMU was a sewing club to make clothing for poor people.

Momma saw to it that Sunday was the Sabbath -- period. Until I was 10 years old, I had to wear my Sunday clothes all day long and couldn't play outside or ride my bicycle and most certainly could not go to a movie. All of those were sins on the Sabbath. God was somehow keeping score, and Momma was definitely keeping tabs. The Reverend Cecil Perry, our Baptist preacher, was often seen standing outside the Ritz Theater on Sunday afternoons taking down names of any young Baptists who were going into the Sunday movie and reporting it to their parents. I cannot imagine Momma's reaction if she ever got a call from Reverend Perry saying I was going into a Sunday movie. Reverend Perry was an absolute deterrent for me.

The Baptists of the county organized themselves into a Butler County Baptist Association and began holding "Fifth Sunday meetings." It turns out that a fifth Sunday in a month occurs about every three months. The various country Baptist churches rotated holding the Fifth Sunday event at their church. It was an honor, and each church went all out. Fifth Sunday meetings lasted all day and involved multiple preachers, all kinds of food laid out on long tables and choirs singing in rotation both inside and outside of the church. After Sunday dinner at noon, I usually took a nap in the back seat of our car while Momma and Daddy attended the afternoon services and choir singings. By late afternoon, we drove back into town, filled with some vague fear of hell, fire and damnation. At that age, I thought "hell" and "fire" were separate concepts. I also wasn't clear on what exactly would lead us to live in hell for an eternity.

I mentioned Daddy's guilt over switching service stations from Gulf to Shell, because it caused hurt feelings for Mister Lane Grass, the Gulf distributor. Aside from his lofty status as one of Greenville's three gas and oil magnates, Mister Lane also sang bass in the First Baptist Church choir -- bad bass, I might add. For years, my brother and I loved to imitate Mister Lane's deep solos. You haven't heard vibrato until you've heard Mister Lane sing bass. When he dipped for the lowest notes, you could count the slow vibrations. What's more, the precise diction of his singing voice bore no resemblance to his ordinary speaking voice. When he spoke, it was pure south Alabama drawl. When he sang, it was like some made-up operatic dialect. If you've ever heard Andy Griffith sidekick Gomer Pyle speak country then sing classically, you have some idea of Mister Lane's odd vocal transformation.

One of my favorites that Mister Lane sang was *How Great Thou Art.*

"O Lord my God, When I in awesome wonder,
Consider all the worlds Thy Hands have made;
I see the stars, I hear the rolling thunder,
Thy power throughout the universe displayed."

And then came the refrain, where Mister Lane turned up the volume and his vibrato:

"Then sings my soul, My Saviour God, to Thee,
How great Thou art, How great Thou art.
Then sings my soul, My Saviour God, to Thee..."

(At this point I could almost hear Mister Lane sucking in air as he prepared to let loose with the last two lines.)

How great Thou aarrrt,
HOW ...GREAT... THOU... ARRRTTTTTTT!!

He delivered that last "art" so long and loud that the stained glass windows trembled. A bit more volume and he would have blown them out. Despite sometimes being off-key, Mister Lane gave a magnificent performance on this hymn. It left me with goosebumps on my arms and neck. He held nothing back when it came to *How Great Thou Art.*

Fried Methodist Chicken And The First...

And like clockwork, every time Mister Lane sang a solo, after the service Daddy would bring up his regrets over having defected from Gulf to Shell.

While the music at the First Baptist Church brings back fond memories, the sermons do not. It wasn't so much the content as the length. If our good Reverend Perry got into it, there was no stopping him. He could go on and on and on. His blatant disregard for the clock wouldn't have been so evident had the First Baptist Church not been surrounded by homes of the Methodists. I always thought this curious, if not intentional on the part of the Methodists. You see, the Methodists always got out of church exactly at noon, drove or walked straight home, took off their Sunday clothes and started frying chicken. With no air conditioning and the windows wide open, all those frying Methodist chickens sent their mouth-watering aromas right toward the First Baptist Church where blowing wall fans sucked the crisp salt-and-peppered goodness right into our sanctuary and under our noses.

Lord. Have. Mercy.

After the chicken got to frying good, you could smell the biscuits baking and then the incredible fragrance of fried okra, green beans simmering in fat-back water and cornbread hot out of the oven. Then worst of all, you could sniff out the exact time they started making the gravy. It was agony. I was sure the Methodists did it on purpose. I pictured them fanning all those delicious aromas toward the First Baptist church and laughing.

Finally at about 12:15, Revered Perry would get to the part where he called for new members to join the church. All who wanted to join were asked to come down front and publicly profess their faith and then the congregation voted them into the fellowship. I never saw anyone voted out but my brother and I always whispered about the possibility, much to the consternation of Momma who told us to hush. She always sat between me and my brother in an effort to keep us quiet. It didn't always work.

As we sat there being tortured by those frying Methodist chickens, I would secretly hope no one would join the church that day. Then I would feel guilty because my stomach was stronger than my faith. In the end, I rarely got my wish. It always seemed that the stronger the aroma of fried chicken, the more people would come down front to profess, and the more people who came down front, the more Reverend Perry would stop the singing and urge more people to come forward. If the odor of frying chicken was overwhelming, he would hold up his hands to stop the singing mid-verse. You could hear the organ moan out a last discordant note followed by Mister Lane holding an off-key bass note too long. Then Reverend Perry would launch into a mini-sermon, calling and urging those who were wavering to come on down front for the final call. There was just something about the smells of frying chicken that brought more people to God in the First Baptist Church ... and, I should add, agony to me and my stomach. I'm convinced there is not a religion on earth that can out-fry the Methodists, especially on a Sunday. To this day, fried chicken is and will always be Sunday Methodist food to me.

I adhered faithfully to the Baptist Church until my early teens. After Mother's death in 1945 just before my 14th birthday, I completely parted ways with all organized religion. I could not reconcile a God who took my mother with one who was loving and kind. I didn't return to the church for 20 years thereafter.

Three

FRISKY

Just as gasoline, religion and civic clubs defined the men of the town, dogs and bicycles defined the boys. Wherever we went, our dogs and bicycles went with us. All we had to do was ride around town until we found the identifiable dogs and bicycles of our friends parked in some front yard.

My dog was Frisky. I got him when I was in the first grade. A family friend from Selma sent him to me in a shoebox by Trailways bus. He was tiny. I fed him with a little milk bottle for a couple of weeks. Frisky was a mixed breed, part fox terrier and we thought part Beagle hound. He was mostly white with black ears and a brown nose. Every day, Frisky walked with me to school and followed me inside. He wasn't a big dog, so he fit right under my feet at my desk. He was the only dog allowed in school. I guess because he started with me in the first grade, the teachers never gave it much thought. From time to time, he would wander outside and just hang around the schoolyard where the other dogs gathered. Then at the end of the day, he followed me home. He didn't know any tricks except to "come" and "sit," but he loved to retrieve balls when I threw them. At night he slept on my bed, despite my mother's early efforts to discourage him. She tried repeatedly to shoo him off, but he would always sneak back in and jump on the bed. She eventually gave up.

Frisky almost never left my side from the first grade until I was in the 12th grade. Sometimes I think he assumed I was his parent.

The only time Frisky was not with me was when some female dog in town went into heat. Frisky was not just a boy dog, he was a boy dog in constant search of female dogs in heat. It was easy to know whenever a female dog went into heat since there would be nearly a dozen male dogs lying around the yard, patiently waiting for the female to come outside. The owner of the house sometimes would try to chase the male dogs away with a watering hose -- to no avail. After a few days, when the female went out of heat, the male dogs would amble back to their home bases.

Frisky was more successful than most male dogs in getting to the females. I remember Daddy getting telephone calls from all over town, some more forthcoming than others: "Tell Clifton that his Frisky just knocked up our dog! He was all hung up and I had to turn the hose on both of them to get them disconnected."

Of course Frisky's sexual exploits did nothing to calm our own boyhood fantasies. As I got older and learned about the birds and the bees, I became increasingly envious of Frisky's sexual freedom. Over the years, more and more small dogs in town began to look like him. He probably had over a dozen sons and daughters in Greenville.

Being promiscuous wasn't Frisky's only claim to fame, however. In 1939 when I was eight years old, the movie *Gone with the*

Frisky

Wind was released. Of course, it didn't get to the Greenville Ritz Theater until a year after that. We were all excited to see it. Frisky, as usual, followed me to the theater but had to stay outside. The Ritz was about the only place in town he couldn't come in. The movie ran a long four hours with an intermission halfway through. When it was finally over, we filed outside and there sat Frisky patiently waiting for me. He had held his post the entire time and was thrilled at my return, jumping up and down and trying to lick me. That four-hour vigil earned him widespread acclaim as Greenville's most faithful dog.

Every Friday afternoon in the fall, the Quarter Million Dollar Black and Gold Greenville High School Marching Band led a parade down Commerce Street heralding the football game that night. Frog, a mentally retarded adult whom you'll hear more about later, marched directly on my right with Frisky just behind him. Neither Frog nor Frisky ever missed a parade. Then later that evening when the band marched on the field at half time, Frisky followed me and joined the show. No one ever objected.

The only people who didn't like Frisky were the country boys who taunted me about what a "sorry" dog he was. "That dog ain't worth nothin'... Can't hunt... What's he good for 'cept to eat and sleep?" they'd say. Other country boys would jump in, "Sorry-ass city dog. Wouldn't know a possum or rabbit if he saw one." Sometimes they continued until I got mad. If it got really heated, I would end up in a fight, city boys versus country boys. More than once, the principal or a teacher had to break up a brawl defending Frisky's honor.

Frisky died when I was a senior in high school. He was killed in a dog fight with a neighbor's two Chinese chows. His insides were hanging out and he was barely breathing when I found him. I had to carry him to the veterinarian to have him put down. It was one of the saddest days of my life. I seriously thought about shooting both chows and would have, but Daddy talked me out of it. I buried Frisky in a grave in our backyard among Daddy's camellia bushes.

I never had another dog until years later when I married, but no dog ever measured up to Frisky's effect on me. For years I kept a framed photograph of Frisky on my dresser. Recently, I got my wife Ann to do an oil portrait of him. Now it hangs above my desk.

Four

BILLY

In the summer after the first grade, just before I turned 7, we moved to a rental house on South Park Street. Mamie, our cook, lived about three blocks away to the south in Baptist Hill, one of the black sections of town. She walked to and from home to our house, where she cooked and helped Momma clean house.

Billy was one of Mamie's children. He was about a year older than I. We became immediate friends. Billy would follow Mamie to work, and we would play together in my backyard. I guess Momma didn't think too much about my playing with Billy at first.

Billy made the best rubber guns in town. These were wooden guns that shot long, elastic rubber bands cut from old inner tubes. He cut them out of wooden crates he found out back of the grocery store, shaping them into rifles and pistols. Then the rubber band was stretched from the tip of the gun back to a notch on the handle. There was a string underneath the rubber band so when you pulled up the string it released the rubber band as a bullet.

He preferred truck inner tubes over car inner tubes, since the rubber was thicker and more powerful. The truck rubber bands traveled much farther. Billy's rubber guns could shoot over 20 yards, a longer distance than any other rubber guns. He had invented a special wooden stock into which he cut several notches so the guns could release up to four rubber bands at a time, almost like a machine gun.

Billy and I formed a small army with two other boys. We played cowboys and Indians almost every day, holding off the other small-boy armies in the neighborhood with Billy's rubber guns. Billy was the only black boy in the bunch, but we didn't care since he made and shared his fine rubber guns. At our young age, we had no idea we were violating a taboo.

As the summer passed, all of us learned to ride bikes which became horses in our games of cowboys and Indians. Billy could ride with both hands free, driving the handle bars with his knees while shooting his rubber gun. He was something special.

Billy was spending more and more time at our house. He and I built a small wooden shack in the backyard as our official headquarters. We often ate lunch together. By the end of summer, Billy was my best friend. We were nearly inseparable.

One night, I heard Momma and Daddy talking in their bedroom down the hall from my room. "Mabel," I heard Daddy say in a quiet voice. "You do know the neighbors are beginning to talk about Billy and Clifton playing together."

I couldn't hear what Momma replied, but the next day just before I started back to school in the second grade, I overheard Momma and Mamie in a hushed conversation. I sneaked closer outside the kitchen door to hear what they were talking about.

"Mamie, you do know the neighbors are talking about Clifton and Billy playing together," Momma said. "You do know that is not going to come to any good."

Billy

Mamie kept washing the dishes. She only said, "Yassum," almost whispering.

Momma went on. "I hate it but we've got to separate them. Sooner or later, one of the white men is going to do something mean. I feel it in my body."

Mamie turned to look at Momma. Her face was a deep sad. Tears ran down her cheeks and her mouth twisted as she fought back crying. "I knows. I knows," was all she said. Momma was crying, too.

I waited in dread for Momma to tell me. I ran out into the backyard to hide. She called out from the back door for me to come in. I knew what was coming. Momma had me sit on her bed in her bedroom. She had a long face. Her eyes were red from crying. "I know you like to play with Billy," she began, "but I'm afraid you have to stop. Billy is a good boy. But..." She stopped for several moments. "But you know black people live with black people and white people live with white people...that's the way it is. It's the law."

I went out to the wooden shack that Billy and I built. I sat there a long time staring at Billy's rubber guns he had given me. I would never play with Billy again. Momma laid down the law. Frisky crawled into my lap and licked my face. He knew exactly how I felt.

From time to time, I saw Billy pedal up the street on his bike on his way to town. I waved at him but he never looked at me, never waved, just kept pedaling. I heard years later that he had gone to Detroit with Mamie and the other members of the family. They were part of the black exodus to Detroit for work in the automobile factories in the 1940s. I have always wondered what happened to him.

At that time, the day I lost Billy was the saddest of my life.

Five

JOHN

John Sherling was the first boy I met in kindergarten when we moved to Greenville in 1936. Charles Chambliss was the second. As soon as we met, the three of us ran out to the playground in the back of Miss Frances's house and began swinging on the swing set. We were together from that day on.

When I first visited John at his home, he took me to the family den. We were both five years old. Miss Katie Lane, John's mother, was there with his grandmother Miss Kate and Francis the black maid. We called all the white women "Miss" in the same fashion we called white men "Mister." "Miss" simply became part of the first name. Miss Katie Lane's full maiden name was Miss Katie Lane Kendrick, daughter of old Doctor John Kendrick. She was married to Mister Dan Sherling, John's father. Her married name was Miss Katie Lane Sherling.

There was a picture of John hanging on the wall of the den. I could not tell if it was a drawing or a photograph. I asked, "Is that picture took or drewed?" The women laughed and then kept laughing. Miss Katie Lane called me "Took-or-drewed" from then on.

Clifton K. Meador M.D.

John came from an old Greenville family. His grandfather "Old Doctor John," as everyone called him, was a legend. Young John's appointed role in life was to follow in his late grandfather's footsteps and become a fine doctor, too. It did not happen. It did not come even close, as you will see.

From the start, John seemed to have it all. In his childhood, he had five women who doted on his every wish. There were two black women – his personal nurse Francis and Mazz the family cook and maid. Then there was Miss Edna, an old maid great aunt, sister of his grandmother. Next came his grandmother, Miss Kate, widow of Old Doctor John. And finally there was his mother, Miss Katie Lane. From what I could observe through the years, the major focus of all these women was to get John raised and educated so he could become like his legendary grandfather. Long shadows of successful dead ancestors are sometimes crippling. Old Doctor John's legacy was weight enough to carry; add five doting women and you have some understanding of John's course in later life.

There was one other male in the family. That was John's father, Mister Dan Sherling, the Shell Oil distributor for the entire county. It was my father's friendship with Mister Dan that led him to switch from Gulf to Shell. As Daddy said repeatedly, he took on a lifetime of guilt for forsaking Mister Lane Grass and Gulf gasoline.

As soon as puberty arrived, John forgot everything in life except girls and fast cars. At age 15, he got full use of the family Oldsmobile, the fastest passenger car in existence at the time. The '46 model was one of the first cars produced following the war. It was a magnet for teenage girls and, in later life, for all sorts and varieties of women. It was a major contributor to his continued downward fall.

John was eternally happy and even-spirited. We never fought or argued. I never saw him mad. Often I came along on his family

John

trips as his companion. His father, also eternally happy and cheerful, took us all over Florida from St. Augustine to Daytona Beach to Cypress Gardens and down to Tampa. They also took me on trips to Montgomery and Birmingham. I was like a brother for John.

I think part of John's affinity for me came from his mother, Miss Katie Lane. I had decided I wanted to become a doctor after my fifth birthday when I had severe pneumonia and was in a coma for two weeks. This was all before antibiotics were discovered. After that near-death experience, I never wavered in my desire to go into medicine. Miss Katie Lane knew that, and I think she hoped my drive would rub off on John. It didn't.

By everyone's opinion, John was handsome from his early childhood. In his teenage years, he became a magnet for pretty girls. Sometimes two or three at a time were after him. Between fast cars and pretty women, there was not much room left for serious study.

One of the things that constantly lured John was Jack Casey's speed record from Greenville to Montgomery set at 32 minutes and 23 seconds. He talked about it constantly. As soon as he got his driver's license at age 15, he became obsessed with beating that record.

Jack Casey was a volunteer firemen and movie projectionist at the Ritz Theater. Jack had spent a few years in Hollywood working odd jobs, trying to make it in the movies. Failing, he returned home to Greenville and got a job at the Ritz. His claim to fame was that he once shook hands with Betty Grable. Jack never got over Hollywood. He wore jodhpurs, knee-high boots and a beret set on the side of his head. Jodhpurs, designed as riding pants for horsemen, were generous around the hips and thighs and tight from the knee down. Many movie directors wore them for effect.

Clifton K. Meador M.D.

Hollywood aside, Jack was most famous for his fast driving, especially that speed record from Greenville to Montgomery.

One Sunday in October of 1947, John pulled up to my house. "Jump in," he said. "Got it all planned in my mind. Ran the course to Montgomery last week. Think I can beat 32 minutes and 23 seconds. Let's go." With that we were off to the north of town on US 31. The unofficial official race course ran from the entrance of the Greenville Country Club to the Southern Dairy Plant just south of Montgomery -- around 40 miles.

John gave me a stopwatch to record his time. I was in the passenger seat, ready to ride. He got a running start. By the time we passed the official starting point, John was already doing 80 mph. I clicked the stopwatch as we passed the country club. We were off.

U.S. Highway 31 between Greenville and Fort Deposit to the north was all curves. John entered each one as far to the edge of the inside lane as possible and then slid across into the other lane as he negotiated the curve, sometimes running on the rims of his tires, screeching and sliding and often off onto the shoulder or even into the ditch on the other side of the curve. At one point, I saw an old man up ahead standing on the right shoulder of a steep curve. I just knew John was going to hit the man. There was no way not to. Somehow we miraculously missed him. As we passed I saw the man's face directly outside my front window no more than a few feet away. His face was as clear as if he were looking through a glass door – an expressionless face suspended in time, like a black-and-white photograph.

After we passed through the small town of Fort Deposit, I knew we had a chance to break Jack Casey's record. Most of the road on in to Montgomery was straighter. But then we had our closest call. I saw a wagon being pulled by a mule over a mile ahead. As we approached the wagon, a car topped the hill ahead of the wagon, heading straight toward us. We would either hit the wagon from behind or if we veered around to pass the wagon we would hit the oncoming car head on. John did neither. He swerved the car off to the right of the wagon onto the shoulder of the road and into a shallow ditch. We bumped and bounced and swayed as we passed the wagon on its right. Then we swerved back, fishtailing onto the asphalt road and into the outskirts of Montgomery. That's when I saw the Southern Dairy Plant up ahead. I began to count down the seconds. At exactly 31 minutes and 20 seconds we passed the dairy plant – a new record and lasting fame for John. The preacher even mentioned John's unbroken speed record at his funeral 54 years later.

I never again entered the barbershop for my haircut without Mister Diamond the barber or someone asking me about the ride to Montgomery with John. I told the story over a dozen times, basking in the associated fame.

John had no fear of crashing. One time he and I drove to Pensacola to a house party at the beach. On the way from Pensacola to Fort Walton, we came onto a long straight stretch of road. A Greyhound bus pulled up behind us, blowing the horn as a signal to pass us. John started playing tricks. He sped up just as the bus started to pass so it had to drop back in the lane. Then when the traffic got heavy coming at us, John slowed down to a crawl which made the bus driver lay on his horn even more. As soon as the oncoming traffic thinned, John sped up again so the bus couldn't pass. This went on and on. Slow then fast, fast then slow. I knew that any minute we were going to die. Soon we hit a very long stretch of straight road, so John sped up. Both John and the bus were now going 90 miles an hour. I pleaded with him to cut it out. Finally, he slowed and pulled over to let the bus pass. As it did, the red-faced bus driver shook his fist at us. John just laughed. I may have been in terror of being run off the road and killed, but John loved every minute.

Clifton K. Meador M.D.

John divorced his only wife early in life and never remarried, starting a series of affairs with dozens of different women. He often brought them with him when he came to visit me. He seemed to want my opinion about the women or maybe he did it to show off. He often told me what he liked in particular about the different women he dated. One had hips like Marilyn Monroe. Another had breasts like Jane Russell. There was a brunette whose hair reminded him of Vivien Leigh. He had a thing for movie stars. He liked the hair and eyes of Rita Hayworth. Doris Day had such a sweet face. His all-round favorites were Elizabeth Taylor and Grace Kelly.

His problem was that eventually he found some part of each woman he was dating that he didn't like. He seemed to have a composite of desirable features that he required in all his women and, sooner or later, they all failed in one or more of these, there being no perfect woman in his eyes. The slightest imperfection would begin to wear on him and ruin the relationship. I sometimes thought he must have formed some perfect image early on in his mind that he could never find in real life. I never really got to the bottom of his difficulties with women. I kept coming back to his childhood and those five women who doted on his every move. I wondered how any one woman could ever replace the full and undivided attention of five.

Despite all of his faults, John remained my lifetime friend. Like all old friends, we could be apart 10 years at a time and then take up again like we had never been separated. He was such good company, the best storyteller I ever knew.

Six

CHARLES

I also met Charles Chambliss in kindergarten. Like with John, we too became immediate friends. It just happened.

Charles was a calm person. We often read books together. One of our favorite writers was Robert Benchley, a comic writer who wrote many funny stories. We often sat on his screen porch and rotated reading Benchley aloud, falling out laughing. We also shared comic books and Big Little Books. A Big Little Book was a small square block of a book with pictures and stories, mostly Westerns about cowboys and robbers.

Another common bond with Charles was his ability to write humor. Each year in junior and senior high, the school held a skit night. Each grade had to write and perform a short play. There were six in all, one for each of the six grades. A jury awarded a prize for the best. Charles and I wrote five skits together and then produced and directed them. We won first prize for three of those years.

It didn't take much of an idea to stir us into making up a story. One year, we had heard that Julius Caesar had epileptic fits.

Clifton K. Meador M.D.

Somehow in some slightly sick manner, that struck us as funny. So we set the scene. The entire skit was nothing but a prolonged slapstick seizure by the character dressed in a toga playing Caesar. We made the whole thing up, nothing resembling Shakespeare. By the time Caesar had knocked over all the props, the audience was wild with laughter.

Another time we saw a box of wine-tipped cigars in the downtown drug store. The idea of a wine-tipped cigar was funny enough, but the idea of the cast acting drunk on wine-tipped cigars was irresistible. The audience loved it, too. It didn't take a lot of imagination to get laughs in junior high school.

One of the advantages of being friends with Charles was the location of his house. He lived directly across the street from Isabel Woolby, my first girlfriend. I kissed Isabel one day when we were sitting on a bench in her backyard. We were both 13 years old. She was the first girl I ever kissed. It fired off all sorts of indelible feelings. It was like my entire brain was reprogrammed in an instant. I discovered the meaning of "head over heels in love." When I told Charles about the kiss, he went, "Oh gad, why would you want to kiss a girl?" He made "ugh" faces. It was not long however before he told me he had kissed Caroline Smithers one night at her birthday party.

My love affair with Isabel was short-lived, although it took me a long time to get over her. Her mother was a religious fundamentalist and so was the entire family – husband, her son Sid and her three daughters, including Isabel. Isabel insisted I go to church with her if she were going to see me at all. The church was some Pentecostal branch out on the edge of town. But before I could decide, her mother called me into the living room. She told me that because I was a Baptist and therefore a non-believer she could not let me see Isabel anymore. "Just stay away from Isabel," were her exact words. I thought my world had come to an end. I could

Charles

hardly pedal my bike back home. After a few weeks in the dumps, I got an idea as to how I might regain ground with Isabel.

Isabel was close to her brother Sid. Sid played trombone. In fact, he played first chair and I played second chair trombone in the band. I thought if I could really get to be outstanding on the trombone like her brother, then Isabel would somehow get over her religious objections and begin to see me again. I even thought she would transfer her affection for her brother to me.

The state band festival and music competition was coming up in the fall in Tuscaloosa. I had all summer to practice and I did. I mowed neighbors' yards in the morning and practiced trombone every afternoon, three and four hours at a session, five days a week. I had dreams of becoming the number one trombone player in the state of Alabama. If I could do that then Isabel would fall so in love with me that she would disobey her mother and be my girlfriend. Of course I told no one of my plan, not even Charles or John.

Each year the music competition was held in Tuscaloosa at the University of Alabama. The entire Quarter Million Dollar Greenville High School Black and Gold Marching band went to the competition. This particular year, we got a commendation but didn't win a numbered place in the contest. Charles and I were the only ones who entered the individual competition.

Charles had hardly practiced his clarinet. He didn't need to. He had extraordinary musical talent. Near genius level. Could play any tune by ear. He played Dixieland music, jazz, popular and the classics. There was no clarinet music he couldn't play at first sight. Of course, Charles won first place, making him the number one clarinet player for the whole state of Alabama. Charles was the best, and it did not faze him. Whereas John constantly searched for affirmation and excitement, Charles was completely comfortable in himself. He had a true natural gift of music that I envied.

I didn't fare so well, however. I turned out to be ranked the seventeenth trombone player in the state. Seventeenth! Not first or even second. Seventeenth! After all summer practicing every day, I was only the seventeenth. I knew then that I was not musically talented. It would be the only time in my life that I would go all-out at something and then know with certainty it was not for me.

As strange as it may seem, after the shock wore off, the experience left me with a strange calm. I knew something about myself I had not known before. It also eventually put my desire for Isabel out of my mind, even though I always thought she was the prettiest girl I knew.

Charles and I played in a dance band for the rest of high school, doing gigs on the weekends with a larger local band. Charles went on to become an orthodontist. He continued his music, forming and leading his own small bands, playing local gigs on nights and weekends the rest of his life. He remained a top musician, often playing Dixieland or jazz with the best musicians whenever he went to New Orleans.

After John's funeral, Charles and I traveled around town together, telling old stories. I thought about the contrasting personalities of Charles and John, as different as two people can be. Each somehow fed a different part of me. I drew excitement and adventure from John and envied his ability to attract women. I drew the love of humor, reading and writing from Charles and cherished his extraordinary gift of music.

With John now dead, Charles remains my best and oldest friend.

Seven

World War II

World War II loomed over my childhood from 1941 to 1945. It was in the background of every day, never out of mind. The uncertainty of the war permeated every corner of our lives. The town of Greenville, Butler County, the state of Alabama and the entire nation turned its attention and efforts toward the war. We were united like I would never see again in my lifetime. We were the people of the United States of America.

It all started for me one chilly Sunday afternoon as I pedaled my bike back from throwing footballs with Charles. Daddy had finally persuaded Mother to relinquish her "no playing on Sundays" rule. I think he warned her she was raising a sissy if she didn't let up. I had turned 10 in September, and that day my brother Dan was turning 15. The date was December 7, 1941 -- Pearl Harbor Day.

As usual, we had gone to Sunday School and then to the morning church service. That afternoon, as I pedaled my bike toward home, I saw a woman in the distance come out on her front porch and start waving her arms and yelling. I couldn't understand what she was saying. When I got closer, I heard, "It's the Japs! The Japs! Bombed Pearl Harbor! Sneak attack!" She kept screaming the words, announcing it to her world with no one to listen but me. I waved at her and raced home to find Momma, Daddy and Dan huddled around the radio in our living room.

We listened most of the afternoon as the static-filled news came in from Hawaii. After first, it sounded like the Japs had completely destroyed our entire Pacific fleet. The news got more and more detailed and more serious. Daddy kept shaking his head from side to side as the awful news spilled forth.

The Monday after Pearl Harbor, the principal called us to the auditorium where we listened to President Roosevelt's famous radio speech. He called the attack "a day of infamy." Indeed it was, and it forever changed the carefree world of my small Alabama town. From that day forward, the war was everywhere.

Gasoline was rationed by the summer of 1942. Each car had an A, B or C sticker on the windshield. The majority of cars sported A stickers, which meant they were only allowed four gallons a week. At 25 cents a gallon, that came to $1 a week. Daddy got a preferential C sticker because his job required both train and car travel.

Soon meat and butter were rationed. Then coffee. Then sugar. As a young boy I missed chewing gum and candy most, due to sugar rationing. I never did figure out what chewing gum did for the war effort. Women complained about the absence of silk hosiery. Dress shirts also disappeared, and cigarettes became scarce. Pretty much anything you could think of was in short supply, being redirected to the war.

By early 1942, we began to practice air raid drills for both day- and nighttime attacks, at first nearly every month. Daddy was the air raid warden for about two blocks. He had a helmet and arm band. Dan was his assistant warden, and he got a helmet and arm band, too. I envied that. At night when the air raid siren sounded,

World War II

Momma and I sat in the dark living room and waited until the all-clear siren sounded. Daddy went from house to house getting the neighbors to draw their shades or turn out their lights. At school, when the siren sounded for the drill, we had to climb under our desks and duck our heads to the floor.

You might think all this talk of war would have been frightening. Not for me and Dan and our friends. It was the most exciting thing we could think of. I loved the drills. I delighted in pretending we were about to be under attack, even secretly wished for it. It never occurred to me that Greenville was not a strategic war target for the Nazis or Japs. We were 150 miles inland from the Gulf of Mexico with nothing vital for the enemy to target. There was no way for German or Japanese planes to be anywhere near us, but that didn't keep us from hoping. The U.S. Government printed booklets showing silhouettes of German and Japanese fighter planes and bombers, which we quickly learned to identify. Every day, we kept our eyes trained on the sky. Charles and I built an extensive collection of model airplanes out of balsa wood and tissue paper. It included most of the U.S., German and Japanese planes and hung from the ceiling of Charles's bedroom. Any time we heard a plane pass over, we rushed outside hoping it was a Japanese Zero fighter or maybe a German Messerschmitt. We were always disappointed.

There were a few instances that brought the war closer to our little town, fueling our boyhood imaginations. The first was when a German submarine was sunk in the Gulf of Mexico, outside the mouth of Mobile Bay about 150 miles from Greenville. News of the sub's existence and demise increased the anxiety level immediately. When they raised the sub, they found theater ticket stubs for a Mobile picture show in the jackets of some of the dead sailors. German sailors had obviously sneaked into Mobile to see a movie. With this news, any and all strangers who happened into Greenville became possible German spies. Our fantasies went wild.

Then in 1944 the government built a German prisoner-of-war camp a few miles north of town. It housed around 100 German POWs. These men were put to work clearing underbrush and cutting timber in the large pine forests south of town near Chapman, so every weekday their caravan of open-body trucks passed through the streets of Greenville. We loved to stand at attention as the trucks passed by and mimic the "Heil Hitler" salutes we saw in the war movies and newsreels. The POWs laughed, waved and often threw German magazines and books to us. Somehow we did not harbor the same hatred for the Germans that we did for the Japanese.

My brother Dan, now 17, had acquired quite a fake German accent from watching all the war movies. One night, he and a group of his buddies had the insane idea to drive up to the POW camp and call out in a German accent to the guards. They pulled up to the secured area and, in his best accent, Dan asked permission to visit one of the POWs. "Vee are here to see Herr Frederick fon Junger-mann," Dan yelled. "Vill you bring Herr fon Junder-mann to zee gate?"

As you can imagine, searchlights flooded the car. Sirens sounded. Armed guards swarmed around them, demanding everyone get out with hands up and lie face down on the ground. Finding it was a hoax, the commander of the prison camp telephoned Mister Gus, Greenville's dreaded police chief who was more than happy to deliver the errant boys back to their angry parents. Dan lost driving privileges for a long time, but he got a lot of mileage out of the story. It made him a celebrity at school, with everybody asking him to tell it over and over. Each time, the tale got more colorful and Dan's German accent got thicker.

The war saturated our every day. It filled the radio, newspapers, weekly newsreels at the movie and every barber shop and café conversation. The various battles became a daily litany repeated over

World War II

and over -- Guadalcanal... Iwo Jima... Guam... Wake Island -- battle after battle in the Pacific. Early in 1942, we heard the awful news from the Philippines about the collapse of Corregidor and Bataan. Then we saw pictures of the Japanese-imposed death march from the Bataan Peninsula that tortured and killed hundreds of Americans. Two native-son brothers from Greenville died on that death march, bringing the horrors of war close to home and intensifying our hatred of the Japanese.

News from Europe was slower in coming. Early on, we heard about the persecution of the Jews by Hitler, but it was much later before we saw the horrible pictures of emaciated Jews and others in the concentration camps. Soon enough, our feelings toward the Germans became as intense as toward the Japanese.

Despite -- or maybe because of -- these atrocities, all of us wanted to get into the war. We were so excited when we heard that the Army Air Force was going to put on a mock-battle show at the small local airfield. We were going to see real paratroopers in action. We took our places among the several thousand people gathered and watched as the planes flew low over the field and then, one after another, dropped dozens of parachuting soldiers. At first, the men looked like a scattering of small flowers in the sky. The closer they came, we could begin to make out soldiers suspended under their giant floating canopies. Then they landed right in front of the crowd, as the Army band struck up marching music. When they hit the ground, the paratroopers unslung their rifles and started firing blanks as they ran across the field toward an imaginary enemy. Our hearts raced being so close to the "action." We could imagine ourselves in the midst of battle as never before. You could feel the crowd's excitement during the entire show, which concluded with the band playing a rousing *Star Spangled Banner*. I have never felt patriotism as strongly as I did that day. Every hair on my neck and arms bristled. If I hadn't been underage, I would have volunteered right then and there.

Clifton K. Meador M.D.

Many others did volunteer. Adjacent to the field were scores of Army recruiters signing up young men who would soon be 18 and eligible for the draft. When my brother Dan turned 18 in 1944, he, too, was eager to serve. Poor vision kept him from it, however, and he was sick about that. It meant he couldn't go with his classmates to serve the country. Being labeled "4F" -- the classification for "physically unfit for military service" -- was something Dan never got over. When the Korean War started years later, he sought to redeem himself. By memorizing the eye chart, he managed to get a commission in the Army. He was determined to heal the emotional wounds of not going to World War II with his friends.

The war continued relentlessly in both war theaters – European and Pacific. Invasions of Italy then Normandy finally ended the European war in May of 1945. Then in August of that year, the atomic bomb on Hiroshima and a few days later on Nagasaki ended the war with Japan.

This war had been a classic conflict of good versus evil. Unthinkable evil by Hitler in Europe, aiming for the complete elimination of all Jews by horrendous means. Evil in the Pacific by the Japanese inflicting repeated cruelty on our captured prisoners. And standing strong against all that evil were the Allied Powers led by our United States military. There was such a sense of national pride when we watched the newsreels of General MacArthur and the Japanese officers on the deck of the USS Missouri signing the documents of formal surrender on Sept. 2, 1945. The long war was finally over.

Eight

Leon and Pearl

As I said in the introduction, Greenville was a two-whore town. There was Maw Gooden south of town near Sandy Bottom, and there was Louise who lived on the northern edge of town, whom you will meet later. Louise's daughter was in my class from the first grade until she dropped out just before the ninth grade. Her name was Pearl.

When we were in the sixth grade in 1943, pre-pubertal I might add, Pearl decided to give us boys some anatomy lessons. It may not have been entirely her idea because that was the year Leon Williams came back from his brief stay in the U.S. Army. Leon was 15 years old and had lied about his age, got into the Army and then was let out after six months when his ruse was discovered. Leon had failed several grades because he had to work on his father's farm to plant and pick cotton. Failing grades to help on farms was a common occurrence for many children then. For this reason, there were always some students in each class who were several years older than the rest. Having older boys and girls in our sixth grade class accelerated our learning about the facts of life.

Clifton K. Meador M.D.

Several things about Leon made him a hero to us. Joining the Army was one. All of us dreamed about being in the Army and getting to fly planes or drive tanks or anything just to get in the war. The war movies glamorized combat and painted the Japs and Germans as completely evil. And here right among us was Leon who had actually *been* in that war, albeit only in a camp in South Carolina. Even though he had been kicked out for lying about his age, he was bigger than life to us. He wore his Army shirt every day.

Another thing that attracted us to Leon was his amazing ability to hand-roll cigarettes. Using only his teeth and one hand, he would pull out the cloth pouch of Bull Durham tobacco from his shirt pocket, open the drawstring, pour out the tobacco onto a cigarette paper, pull the drawstring closed, put the pouch back in his shirt pocket, roll the paper around the tobacco, and lick it closed. All with just his teeth and one hand. Most astonishing was how he could strike a wooden match between his thumb and forefinger, also with one hand.

Adding to his magic was the fact that, in the short time he was in the service, Leon got a tattoo. There was a large black dagger dripping red blood on his right forearm. We couldn't take our eyes off of it. And as if all that wasn't epic enough to dazzle our pre-pubescent selves, we learned one more astounding thing: Leon had visited a whorehouse in Charleston, South Carolina. At recess each day, out on the edge of the playground, Leon would squat down in a circle with us, roll a cigarette, smoke and tell his Army stories. (Most of the country boys smoked at recess out of sight of the teachers.) He took the most delight in telling us every detail about his sexual encounters. This was before any of us had even experienced the earliest signs of puberty. Libido was some vague feeling, still well beyond our grasp. But we were about to get our first lesson, thanks to Leon and Pearl.

Leon And Pearl

One day at recess, after constant questioning about sex and about the whorehouse in Charleston, Leon, slightly exasperated at our naïve questions, said, "Alright, I'll get Pearl to show you her poon. 'Course you gonna have to pay her and me to see it."

Here is the way Leon worked it. Miss Ethel always divided the class into three sections. One section worked on math problems. Another section studied geography. The third section moved up to the front of the room where they each read to Miss Ethel. Whenever the reading group started, Leon and Pearl sneaked into the cloakroom, which was a long, narrow room at the back of the class with two open doors on either end, one to enter, the other to exit. It's where we stored coats, hats and other personal belongings. After a few minutes had passed and we were sure Pearl was ready, the rest of us boys would file into the cloakroom one at a time, give Leon a penny, take our peak at Pearl's naked bottom and then sneak out the other end and back to our desk. Only one of us could go at a time to avoid attracting the attention of the stern Miss Ethel Coward.

"Miss Ethel," as we called her, was our sixth grade teacher. She was an old maid, strict, mean and somewhat hard of hearing. She was a force with which to be reckoned. We didn't care, however, when it came to Pearl in the cloakroom. It was worth the risk. If you wanted to get your heart rate up real quick, you took a run through cloakroom, caught a glimpse of a half-naked girl on the way through and sped back to your desk without being caught. As they say nowadays, "It was a rush."

We kept up these shenanigans for a month whenever the weekly reading group moved to the front of the room. Miss Ethel was always up front of the classroom teaching away with the reading group, oblivious to what was going on at the back. Everything was going smoothly until the day one of Pearl's cloakroom customers spotted the broken pipe organ. It was the old kind that operated with pedals and had long been relegated to the back corner of the cloakroom. If you depressed those pedals, there was a brief lag followed by an awful, loud, protracted, groaning, discordant moan. From time to time, someone feeling brave would sneak in the cloakroom, stomp on a pedal, fire off the organ, race back to their seat and watch Miss Ethel explode. We had done the organ trick so often that Miss Ethel declared it an automatic paddling by the principal.

In the midst of Leon's and Pearl's anatomic show, one of the boys decided to add to the excitement by hitting an organ pedal and then rushing back to his desk. That did it. Miss Ethel flew towards the cloakroom like a mad hornet. Then suddenly, from the cloakroom we heard her gasp. It sounded like all the air had just been sucked out of that little room. Clearly, she had discovered what was going on. In a few moments, she led Leon and Pearl by their ears out the door and to the principal's office. All three of their faces registered deep crimson. Leon was expelled for a month. Pearl had to stay home for several days.

Show over.

Nine

FROG

Every small town had a retarded adult. Greenville had three, but Frog was the best known and most popular. There was less sensitivity in those days about the word "retarded." These were times for straight talk. There were no euphemisms or any hint of "political correctness." Retarded was retarded.

All three retarded adults lived open lives among the people of the town. All three had graduated from Greenville High School. Then, it was called a "social promotion." Now they call it "mainstreaming," as if the concept is something new.

Frog's real name was Joseph Carroll. He got the name "Frog" early in life. Even his parents called him "Frog." He was a small person, around 5 feet 4 inches and skinny. His head was disproportionately small with large protruding ears, bulging eyes and a mouth that formed an upside down "U." These features together with his short stature made the nickname an apt one. No one thought of it as cruel or unkind. It was a term of endearment.

Frog was in his early 30s when I was a boy, according to the other men who graduated from the high school in his class. He was a member of the class of 1933 and proudly wore the gold "G" jacket he earned as assistant manager of the basketball team. The team that year made won the Southeast Alabama State Tournament, still the best winning record of any basketball team in the history of the school. The trophy sat proudly in the glass case near the entrance of the old high school before it burned down. Leaning against the trophy was a photo of the team picturing a young Frog to its left. He was sitting on a basketball holding two other balls in front of him. He had a whistle on a cord around his neck, which he continued to wear every day of his life.

It took only a little prompting to get Frog to recall the quarter-final game, which had been played in Ozark.

"Yath, big baw ga…won by two…yath…right thar… right thar… Frog thar."

Frog would pant between phrases and rise up, puff out his chest and look six inches taller whenever he was asked about that game. The memory transported him to another time. He was back in that gymnasium amid all the glory of the final game.

He chain-smoked cigarettes, lighting another off the one he was finishing. Freshly lit, the cigarette would nearly burst into flames when Frog put his full draw on it. All the smoke came pouring out his nostrils, never out of his mouth. He reminded me of cartoon bulls who blow smoke out of their nostrils before they charge.

His parents were well-known, respected members of the community and the First Baptist Church. The family sat off to the right of where my family sat. During church, Frog spent his time rolling string into a ball or looking around. Sometimes he would turn his head completely around to the back and stare at the people in the next row. His mother would grab his face and jerk his head so he was facing front again. That would hold him still for only a few

Frog

minutes before he would turn again. Then another forceful jerk from his mother, and so on. I could sometimes hear her whisper loudly, "Stop that. Look forward. No! No!"

Frog was very much a part of the town. Everyone knew him. He, in some way, recognized most people, although I only heard him call one person by name, and that was George which he pronounced "Jaw." George McStenson ran a small clothing store on Commerce Street. George was a classmate of Frog, had gone off to the war, been seriously injured on Wake Island and medically discharged. As the outstanding fullback of the class of '33, George was already our hero when he went off to war. He came back even more of a hero with his war record. Frog worshipped George and ran to him whenever anyone was teasing too much. When that happened, Frog would tear up, bite his lower lip and say to his tormenters, "Jaw whip yo ass." Then he would pedal off on his bicycle to George's store, angry and mumbling to himself. George never had to intervene but would comfort Frog, patting him on the back. "Frog, now don't let 'em get you down. Come on now, go get yourself some candy." George would hand him a penny or a nickel.

Frog worked his way up and down Commerce Street selling boiled or parched peanuts, depending on the time of the year. For a brief time, he worked at Tom's Drive-in and Bus Station at the top of the hill. He didn't have the skills to take orders, so his job was to carry trays of food and drink out to the drive-in customers.

When he sold his peanuts, he stopped in those stores where he was liked and skipped those where he was teased too much. You could always tell where Frog was by his parked bicycle. The bicycle chain gave him fits. He was constantly getting his right pants-leg caught in it. His mother taped every pair from the knee down into a tight legging arrangement using white adhesive tape. His father added a chain guard, a special covering designed to keep the chain from catching pants legs. But despite all this, Frog would still get tangled up at least once a week.

He also wore a blue work shirt buttoned up to the neck and at the wrists and an old-fashioned wool driving cap pulled down low over his ears. His shoes were high topped and laced up above his ankles.

Planter's Mercantile Store was one of Frog's regular stopping places. Tootsie and Roosevelt ran the feed and fertilizer end of Planter's, and I worked there with them on Saturdays. Whenever either of them saw him coming they would say, "Well, here come Mister Frog." Understand that calling him "Mister" was not belittling or poking fun. Quite the contrary. Calling every white man "Mister" was ingrained in every black man who lived and survived in those segregated days. Tootsie said "Mister Frog" in the same tone and inflexion as he would say "Mister Haywood" or "Mister George" or "Mister John," which he called my friend.

Frog would pedal up to the back door, climb off his bicycle and amble down the ramp into the back of the store. If he wasn't smoking, he would light up, grab the cigarette with a tight fist -- the cigarette poking through his fingers -- take one of his deep drags and snort the smoke out of both nostrils. Frog would stand there looking around until he spotted Tootsie or Roosevelt. "Hey…Wha do? Wha do?" Frog would ask.

"Well if it ain't Mister Frog. How you Mister Frog?" Tootsie would reply.

"Doo foo moo too fah," Frog would say in a loud voice.

It was impossible at times to figure what Frog was trying to say. "Faw dof dat fo too…" Frog launched into a language none of us could decipher, but he always appeared agitated about something.

Frog

"Mister Frog, Mister Frog, can't none of us tell what you tryin' to say," Tootsie would say. "We knows it must be real hard to talk and not be understood by nobody sometimes." He spoke earnestly, not smiling, intent on letting Frog know he was listening.

"Mister Frog, got any of yo peanuts out there?" Tootsie often asked, pointing to the door. Frog would amble out and come back with a bag of boiled peanuts. Tootsie would place coins from a small leather pocket purse into Frog's hand. "Let's see here... one...two...three...four...five...they still a nickel ain't they?" Frog would nod widely and grin and head toward the door, putting the coins in his shirt pocket. "You come back Mister Frog -- anytime, hear?" Tootsie would call after him.

"Po man," Tootsie would say as he stood at the door and watched Frog pedal off down the street. "Po man," Roosevelt repeated, nodding in agreement.

One of Frog's favorite events was the weekly Friday afternoon parade in the fall before home football games. I was, by then, a member of the Greenville High School Black and Gold Marching Band. That was its original name, but by the time I joined, it had a new name. Some reporter had dubbed the University of Alabama marching band the "Million Dollar Marching Band," a heady sum in those days. Someone locally decided that Greenville High School, by comparison, had at least a quarter million dollar marching band. The name stuck. It was a mouthful, but we took it as a huge complement.

On Fridays, the band lined up at the courthouse at the top of Commerce Street. With Chief of Police Mister Gus in his Ford police car in the lead, we would march down the entire length of the street past the railroad underpass at the other end. At the time, I thought the distance was at least a mile or more. Actually, it was only about half a mile. Everyone in Greenville turned out for these parades. From babies to grandparents to town dignitaries, our citizens packed both sides of the street, waving and cheering as we passed.

I played second trombone and marched in the first line of the band, just behind the majorettes. Frog always took the position to my right, my dog Frisky following right behind him. Frog never played an instrument, nor did he have a uniform. He just marched in his regular clothes precisely in that position all the way down Commerce Street. From time to time, someone in the crowd would call out, "Hey Frog!" or "Go Frog!" or "That's the way, Frog!" None of the cheers fazed him. He always stared straight ahead, cap pulled down over his ears, completely expressionless and taking strides that stressed his short legs. I wondered what went on in his mind.

Frog never missed a parade. He didn't miss a fire, either. He was a member of the volunteer fire department. When the town siren sounded off, Frog hopped on his bicycle and headed for City Hall where the fire truck was parked. All the other volunteer firemen spilled out of the businesses where they worked and raced in the same direction, running along the canopied sidewalk in front of all the stores. Frog would be in the thick of it. When he got to City Hall, he would jump on the back of the truck and ride to the fire.

When the siren sounded, all traffic pulled to the sides of the street because in a few minutes Jack Casey, another volunteer fireman, was going to be floor-boarding a 1940 Ford up Commerce Street going over 60 miles an hour. You may recall that Jack held the speed record from Greenville to Montgomery until my friend John broke it some years later. Jack would come roaring up Commerce Street with his left arm hanging out the side window, vaguely reminiscent of some cowboy riding a bucking steer with one hand on the reigns. Driving with his right hand on a steering

Frog

knob, he weaved from one side of the street to the other nosing in between all the stopped cars, tires screeching and horn wide open. Later he installed a car siren under the hood and sounded it full blast as he raced to City Hall. Frog often tried to stop Jack for a ride, but could never get his attention. "Stop, stop…it me…Frog… stop…it me...go too fass...too fass…" Jack kept speeding, never stopping or looking.

One of the lasting memories of my childhood was the large number of fires in town. There was always some house that just burned down or some store or some other building half-scorched. Most of the houses were wooden and heated either with wood-burning fireplaces or potbellied stoves set in a hallway. Almost all the fires were traceable to faulty chimneys or fireplaces. It would be many years before central gas or electrical heating came to town.

The high school burned to the ground when I was in the first grade and had to be rebuilt. The schoolyard became the volunteer fire department's practice field. One Sunday each month, the volunteers gathered, uncoiled the hoses and ran water through them, spraying nearby trees. Then they pointed the hoses skyward sending large streams of water high into the air to the delight of all of us who would run and get under the shower, shouting and laughing as we got soaked. Frog loved these drills. He wore his fire helmet, too big for him, down nearly over his mouth. His oversized yellow fireman's coat hung to the ground. He looked like a 5-year-old wearing his father's suit.

The force of a fire hose is tremendous. It takes three men to control the nozzle. The water at full pressure will knock down a large man and spin him along the ground. One Sunday during drills in the schoolyard, Frog was up in the middle of the hose crew. Humoring him, they let him work as a fourth person. He grabbed the nozzle. Frog was in heaven.

After a few minutes of this, the crew decided to see what would happen to Frog if they let go of the hose. On the count of three, they released the mighty hose and stepped back. It rose like a strange serpent until the nozzle was more than six feet in the air -- with Frog hanging on for all he was worth. He looked like a small doll in a yellow raincoat dangling above the ground. Then the hose started to whip back and forth in the air like a giant kite string. Frog still hung on. The crowd was now laughing and cheering. Suddenly, the hose dipped to the ground and started arcing in free form, pushing Frog along with it. Still, he hung on. People were getting concerned and started yelling for Frog to let go, but he hung on. Finally, after the wild hose had dragged Frog all over the place, someone ran to the hydrant and shut down the water.

Frog picked himself up like those thrown bull riders do in the rodeos, slapped his fire hat to his leg, ambled off to one side, bent over and said, "Dam...dropped ...ma ...ceegrets...dropped...ma... ceegrets." Here he'd been sailed and tossed and dragged, and all he could say was that he'd lost his cigarettes.

The crowd rushed toward him, patting him on the back, laughing and yelling, "Way to go Frog!" "That's the way to show 'em!" "Go to it Frog!" I have never seen Frog so proud. For weeks, people would yell at him when he pedaled by downtown, "Frog, you showed 'em!" Or, "Frog, go to it!" Frog would just duck his head, pedal a little harder and mumble, "Yeah... drop ma ceegrets."

Ten

MISTER BILLY'S MORNING GLORIES

The first time I remember getting into trouble was when I was around 10 years old. I still have mixed feelings about it because I thought what I did was justified, even heroic. Momma and Daddy thought otherwise.

Daddy had an extensive collection of camellia bushes. As I have said, Greenville was known all around Alabama as the Camellia City. Most of the men in town grew camellias. They even had a men's camellia club that put on the camellia competition every February. Daddy was active in the club. They learned to graft fine and expensive camellia species onto cheap scrub plants and do all sorts of other gardening tricks. I don't know of another town where most of the men grow flowers. I think it explains a certain tenderness I always associated with Greenville. Men who grow flowers are unlikely to be mean spirited, even if they embezzle a bank now and then.

Daddy's garden ran from the back of the garage all the way to the end of our lot. He had a wire fence along that side of the property forming a side to two enclosed pens. The back pen was the dog yard where Spot and Point, Daddy's two bird dogs, lived. The other pen directly behind the garage was full of Daddy's camellia stock bushes. His young, grafted camellia bushes ran along the inside of the length of this fence so they could get the early morning sunlight from the east.

This arrangement was fine except that our neighbor on the other side of that fence did not care for a dog yard so close to his backyard. Mister Billy McGowen was also a gardener and spent much time planting and watering and making his yard into a showplace. He had already had a nasty, ongoing fight with his other neighbor on the opposite side of his backyard. That neighbor eventually built a huge, hideous wooden fence nearly10 feet tall down the entire length of the lot to silence Mister Billy's constant complaining. You may recall that Mister Billy was one of the three gasoline distributors in town, selling Sinclair gasoline. The mad neighbor threatened to paint "Gulf Oil" in large letters on the already ugly fence. It was a fight that went on for years. No one really understood the cause for such hostility, especially since it violated the old saying that good fences make good neighbors. Not in this case, however.

So the unhappy Mister Billy turned his attention to our wire fence and his desire to hide our dog yard from the view from his backyard. To do this, he planted a long row of morning glory plants down the length of our fence. Before long, the vines covered the fence and blocked out the morning sun from Daddy's camellia plants. Now Daddy wasn't happy. He constantly complained that those morning glories were stealing his camellias' best sunlight. Over and over, he grumbled about those vines. I listened to this harangue for several weeks, then I decided to take action.

I got up early one morning and got to the fence. I reached through the fence and pinched off the morning glory vines just at ground level. That way I thought it would simulate some bug

Mister Billy's Morning Glories

or insect eating the plant and I wouldn't get caught. I pinched off every single vine down the length of the fence.

By late that afternoon, the morning glories were looking sad and wilted. Mister Billy was out there inspecting each vine. I saw out of the back window of my bedroom that he and Daddy were having a conversation. I was staying out of sight. By the next day, the vines were completely limp and turning brown. In two days, they were dried up and a dull brown. Dead.

The following day, Daddy and Momma called me into the living room for a conference. I don't remember the exact conversation, but it was clear that I was the No. 1 suspect in the morning glories' demise. At first, I denied any knowledge of what they were talking about. I'm sure guilt must have been all over my face. They kept questioning me, and before long I started to cry. That was it. I confessed to the whole caper. But I pleaded that I had done it for a good reason -- to save Daddy's camellias.

They insisted I go over immediately, knock on Mister Billy's door and tell him what I had done. I can still recall the dread of facing him. I knocked on the front door and stood waiting for what seemed like half a day. Then Mister Billy answered the door. "Well, what do you want?" he demanded, his face scowling and mean. He stared down at me, silent. Then he called over his shoulder in a loud voice, "Susan, please come to the door. I think you need to hear this." Now the two of them just stood there frowning at me. Neither said a word. Fortunately, I had memorized what I would say. I took a deep breath, and as fast as I could talk I blurted out my apology for killing their vines. I turned, not waiting for a response, and ran back to my yard. Frisky was right behind me.

I avoided all contact with the McGowens for weeks. But at least I fixed Daddy's camellia problem. Mister Billy never replanted those vines.

Eleven

Mister Gus

Like the fictional Mayberry, Greenville had a two-man police force. Mayberry had Andy Taylor and Barney Fife; we had Mister Gus and Mister Pete.

Mister Gus was chief of police. Greenville didn't have a police headquarters, so if Mister Gus wasn't in his police car driving around town, he was at one of three places – City Hall, the courthouse or the county jail across the street from the courthouse. He had been chief for many years, and he dressed the part. His black army-type cap and a Sam Browne black belt crossing over his right shoulder gave him a military presence. His .45 caliber pistol holstered at his right hip let you know he was ready to shoot whoever disobeyed him. Mister Gus didn't say much. He didn't have to. His staring at you was just short of being shot with his pistol. Just the sight of him could make your mouth go dry.

Mister Pete was just the opposite of Mister Gus. He was peg-legged and slightly senile. We called him "Peg Leg Pete," but never to his face. He always worked night duty, hanging out in the street around the corner near the courthouse. I suppose if anything went wrong, he could call Mister Gus to come help.

Clifton K. Meador M.D.

But not much went wrong. In the 12 years I lived in Greenville, there were no shootings, no murders and no robberies, at least not in the white section of town. There were rumors of knife fights in the black sections, but I never heard of a murder, black or white. There was one suicide, and folks were still talking about that years later. The victim's son was a few years ahead of me in school. No one ever knew any details. Every time I drove by that house, I thought of the suicide. I couldn't comprehend someone killing themselves.

There was only one major crime – an embezzlement at the First National Bank. It was an inside job. The cashier of the bank, Clyde Marrow, stole what was in those days a hefty sum of money. The bank examiners uncovered the crime in their audit. Mister Clyde was our neighbor across the street, so we were especially startled over the news. Well, all of us except Daddy. Over the years, Daddy had noted that the banker's yard was gradually filling with beautiful camellias -- award-winning camellias, in fact. Some of the blooms took top prizes at the annual men's camellia show in February. Daddy kept saying, "I just don't understand how a man working on a salary from a bank can afford all those expensive camellia plants." When the examiners caught up with him, he had been embezzling for 10 years, totaling nearly $15,000. Daddy quickly calculated the value of the fancy camellia bushes and figured that's where almost all of the money had gone.

I never knew the consequences of Greenville's only big crime, because the family packed up and left town immediately. We never saw or heard from them again.

Given that this one embezzlement was about as bad as it got, there wasn't a lot for Mister Gus to do as police chief. But that doesn't mean he wasn't a busy man. Although the times were kinder and gentler than now, I think the absence of crime was in part due to Mister Gus's hovering influence. He drove around

Mister Gus

town constantly in his 1939 Ford police car, checking on everything and everybody -- especially us boys. He often stopped and called us over to his car, no matter what we were doing.

"What you boys up to?" he would say. "I don't want to hear of any trouble. Don't make me have to call your parents. You hear?"

From preteen on, we were scared to death of him. If we saw him coming, we would go in the opposite direction or hide in the nearest bush. Having to talk to Mister Gus terrified us, and we avoided it if at all possible. It wasn't simply that we were kids and he was the town's authority figure. There was more to it. Much of our fear came from the stories we heard the black maids and cooks tell. Their fear of Mister Gus -- or police in general -- seemed justified and real. From an early age, I heard over and over, "Po-leece gon' get you. Po-leece shoot you in the back." To us, that meant Mister Gus and Mister Pete. True or not, the sinister warning was seared into our brains. To this day, whenever I see a police car I still hear the phrase, "Po-leece shoot you in the back."

Despite our fear of Mister Gus, there was an increasing urge to get into the edge of trouble. The urge must be pre-programmed into young boys. At least it was for John, Charles and me. The three of us were constantly looking for different ways to entertain our 10-year-old selves. This was before puberty turned our attention to girls. The search for novel amusement resulted in two episodes, one that nearly got us in trouble and one that got us into serious trouble.

The one that nearly got us in trouble involved waiting for trains to pass under the old wooden bridge near our houses. The railroad tracks ran down a deep gulley through the middle of town, crossing under two wooden bridges. We enjoyed playing on the bridge nearest the school, the one where the boogers congregated at night. In the daytime it was perfectly safe. Boogers only come out at night.

Clifton K. Meador M.D.

I'm not sure which one of us came up with the idea, but we decided it would be fun to see if the three of us could pee off the bridge onto the full length of the passing train. We would wait for the steam engine to pass under us on the bridge, then start peeing in sequence on the train. By peeing in sequence, our goal was to pee down the full length of the train as it passed beneath us. John peed, then Charles and then me. Once we got the idea, we did this frequently. We never had enough pee to get to the end of the train, but we kept trying. One day, the brakeman in the caboose leaned out of his window, shook his fist and yelled at us just before he passed under the bridge. We guessed we must have peed on him at some point to make him so mad.

When the brakeman did that, Charles yelled, "Run! I bet he's going to call Mister Gus!" With that, we jumped on our bicycles and pedaled as fast as we could to John's house. We figured his treehouse was our safest refuge. We all thought Mister Gus could -- and would -- handcuff us and put us in jail if he merely wanted to. He could even shoot us in the back if he had to. Worst of all, we knew he would call our parents and tell them what he found us doing. The thought of Momma hearing that I had been peeing off the bridge made me shudder. We remained huddled in John's treehouse for hours, sure that Mister Gus was in his patrol car out looking for us. He never came, thankfully, and we eventually climbed back down to resume playing. But that didn't include peeing on trains. No, never again. The wrath of that brakeman and our fear of Mister Gus ended that stunt for good.

Our next brush with trouble, a few years later, was far more serious. We were lucky nobody was killed.

John, Charles and I had created a secret hideout in the middle of a field of sage brush. The field filled about five acres, bordered by houses on two sides and streets on the other two sides. The brush was 4- to 5-feet tall, tall enough to hide us and our paths which crisscrossed the field. In the center of the field, we built what we called our "fortress." We dug a trench about 10-feet long, 4-feet wide and nearly 5-feet deep. On the top we put sheets of corrugated tin, and on top of the tin we shoveled dirt. This hidden cave became our army headquarters. We had kerosene lanterns to light the inside. It was our place to crawl in, hide and, best of all, to smoke our rabbit tobacco hand-rolled cigarettes.

We tried smoking just about everything to act big. Real tobacco made us sick, so we avoided cigarettes and turned to odd things like dried tree leaves or even ground coffee. We didn't inhale but just blew the smoke back out of our mouths. Rabbit tobacco was our favorite.

Rabbit tobacco grew wild in our field, with long stems and pale whitish leaves. We dried the leaves in the sun and then rolled them into thick cigarettes, using brown sack paper or sometime newspapers. We had heard that the Indians smoked rabbit tobacco and that added to the mystique, as we hid in our cave and smoked our hand-rolled cigarettes.

One day Charles and I were sitting in our fortress letting our minds go wild in fantasies, as usual. I can't remember whether on this particular day we were under attack from wild Indians or engaged in combat with the Japanese or Germans, but suddenly we heard John's voice outside. It was getting louder and louder. He was yelling, "Get out!! Fire!! Get out!!"

When we crawled out into the open, we saw huge flames all around us. Running out into the field, we realized the whole field was burning. Now at full speed, we made it safely to the edge of inferno. This was scary, but it was also grand excitement. Even though we knew one of us must have inadvertently dropped a lit match or cigarette butt and caused all this, we couldn't tear ourselves away. We joined the crowd that was gathering to watch the scene unfold. In a few minutes the volunteer Greenville fire department appeared.

The flames were now lapping up against the houses on the north side of the field. We could see a disaster forming right in front of our eyes, imagining the row of houses going up in flames. The volunteer firemen were dragging heavy fire hoses to the hydrant and spraying water on the sides of the houses. This kept the flames at bay and saved the houses. Within 30 minutes, the danger had passed. The fire in the field pretty much burned itself out, but the firemen turned the hoses on the smoldering sagebrush stubble just to be safe. They watered down the entire field. That's when they found our headquarters.

The fire chief called out, "Looks like some boys were in here up to no good. Got some sort of cave."

The large crowd of people who had gathered on the sides of the street to watch the spectacle were slow to disburse. Not only had the firemen found our hideout, we were about to be humiliated in front of half the community.

As if things couldn't get any worse, about that time Mister Gus showed up in his 1939 police car. We could hear him questioning the fire chief. "You say you think it was a bunch of boys? Got any names?"

We said nothing. Exchanging furtive glances, the three of us turned quietly to find our bicycles and hopefully race off home before somebody pointed a finger.

Too late. Just then, Charles's mother walked up behind us.

"What you boys up to?" she asked with one of those motherly, guilt-assigning looks on her face. "You boys set that fire, didn't you?"

Mister Gus

We were covered in dirt and smelled of smoke, not to mention having full-blown guilty faces covered in soot. We didn't answer at first. We looked at each other sheepishly, wondering what to do. Our silence was as telling as a confession.

"Well?" Charles's mother insisted. "You look guilty to me."

After a moment, Charles, barely audible, said, "Just happened. All of a sudden."

"Well!" she said to John and me, now a fully-in-charge mother. "I am going to call your mothers. Go on home right now!"

The three mothers must have held a telephone conference. By the time I got home, Momma was standing at the front door. "Well, I hear you nearly burned down some houses." she began. "Charles's mother said she thought you had been *smoking?!?* Just you wait until your father hears all of this." I stared at the floor, looking up only once to see a face empty of any expression -- her full Presbyterian face.

The mothers had already decided that we had to go to each house that bordered on the field and confess we had been smoking rabbit tobacco and say we were sorry to have caused all that trouble. But that wasn't the worst of it. After we apologized to those homeowners, we then had to find Mister Gus and confess to him.

We decided to face Mister Gus first then the homeowners. The three of us got on our bikes and headed toward the courthouse. We had drawn straws to see who would do the talking. Charles lost the draw. After riding around for awhile, we found Mister Gus parked in front of the post office.

We jumped off our bikes and walked up to his car. "Hey, Mister Gus!" Charles called out in a super-friendly voice. Charles talked a while trying to minimize the whole situation, while Mister Gus just shook his head. I don't remember all that was said because my entire brain went numb in his presence. He took down our names in his little book and promised to keep us under close observation. He said he wouldn't put us in jail this time, but we could be sure that he would check on our apology to the homeowners "who you boys nearly burned up."

After we left Mister Gus we rode out to the burned field and the surrounding houses and made our apologies, a blur in my memory.

Soon the story was all over town. For months, every time I got a haircut, I had to listen to Mister Diamond, my barber, tell the story over and over to his audience. "Well, here comes Clifton! You boys set any more fields on fire?" This always drew a laugh from the men waiting for haircuts. All I could do was turn red and nod. I confess the whole thing gave me mixed emotions. On one hand, I felt guilty. On the other, I rather enjoyed the notoriety.

Twelve

THE TRAINS

The daily trains that ran north and south were a constant and reassuring feature of life in Greenville. For us boys, they held a great mystique. They signified a connection to the world beyond. Like today's astronauts, the engineers driving those huge engines were our heroes.

Access to the trains on the main line was the reason my father moved our family to Greenville. His job with the Louisville and Nashville Railroad -- better known as the L&N -- required him to travel up and down the railroad line from Nashville to Biloxi, MS. Daddy's job broadly was to do anything to increase agricultural and livestock production in the states of Alabama, Florida and Mississippi. His title was agricultural development agent for the L&N railroad. The theory was that the more the farmers grew and produced, the more the railroad would haul as freight. He spent much of his time with county agents around the state, 4-H clubs and all of the agricultural extension services out of Auburn. He was a goodwill representative of the L&N railroad. It was a wonderful job for him since his interests had no limits.

Clifton K. Meador M.D.

Before we moved from Selma to Greenville, Daddy practiced as a veterinarian. At the depth of the Depression his income fell below $85 a month. After operating on a cow, he told a farmer that his fee was $5 dollars. The farmer said, "Hell, the whole cow's not worth $5." That's when Daddy started looking for other work.

Daddy graduated from Cornell Veterinary College in 1910 and from Auburn in horticulture in 1906. There were no veterinary colleges in the South in those days, so he had to go north to find one. His previous life as a practicing veterinarian and his degree from Auburn in horticulture made him ideally suited for his work with the railroad. I sometimes traveled with him to cattle, dog, sheep, chicken and pig shows where he often served as a judge. His goal was to meet as many people as possible. He was always introduced as "Dr. Meador of the L&N railroad."

Daddy had more names than anyone I ever met. His full name was Daniel John Meador, Jr. Momma called him "John." His classmates from Auburn called him "Dan." His siblings called him "Leedy" (I never discovered why). Momma's three brothers nicknamed him "Zeke." Everybody else called him "Dr. Meador," "Doc Meador" or just "Doc."

Daddy loved the traveling and the work with farmers. He secretly always wanted his own farm. He especially enjoyed the travel by train. All the trains in those days were steam-driven locomotives fueled by coal. Diesel engines came later after the war. The locomotives required large amounts of water to make steam, so the L&N owned a small pond north of town for the sole purpose of supplying the engines with water. Charles and I used to visit that pond to shoot frogs and turtles along its banks.

The trains passed directly through the center of town in a deep ravine that was crossed at two points by wooden bridges. The bridges connected the two main parts of town that would have otherwise

The Trains

been separated by the gully. As a boy, I never understood the expression "from the wrong side of the tracks," because there was no wrong side of the tracks in Greenville. I had friends on both sides.

Growing up in such a provincial small town, I tended to think life on earth revolved around Greenville. A good example was my take on how the L&N trains got their numbers. The odd-numbered trains always ran south, and the even-numbered trains ran north. That was a fact. But coincidentally, train No.1 on its way to Mobile always arrived in Greenville around 1 p.m., and No. 4 heading to Montgomery arrived at 4 p.m. So, of course, I believed for years that the men at L&N headquarters in Louisville, KY, had numbered the trains by what time they arrived in tiny Greenville, Alabama. It made perfect sense to me. How geo-centered can a small town boy get?

Daddy knew every train, freight or passenger, either by number or name. We often sat on our screen porch and heard the trains coming through town. Each time, he would call out their names or numbers or sometimes both. The express trains never stopped in Greenville, roaring on through at top speed. One express freight train passed through town around 10 p.m. every night. No matter what else was happening, on hearing that distant whistle Daddy would say, "There's the Bullet." The Bullet's lonesome, wailing whistle would pierce the night several miles before it reached town, grow loud as it passed on through and then fade in the distance. I heard Hank Williams sing this folk song on the radio, and it stuck in my memory:

In the pines, in the pines where the sun never shines
And you shiver when the cold wind blows.
The longest train I ever saw
Went down that Georgia line,
The engine passed at six o'clock
The caboose went by at nine.

Clifton K. Meador M.D.

In later years, I traced the origin of the song to its first recording in 1926 by Dock Walsh. Through the years words were added or deleted in many different versions. The words I memorized were the same as now sung by Dolly Parton. Those words bring haunting memories of the Bullet and Daddy.

Passenger trains were either local, meaning they stopped at nearly every town, or they were express, stopping only at Mobile to the south and Montgomery and Birmingham to the north. In order to catch an express, you had to ride the local to Montgomery and transfer trains. There were two expresses – the Hummingbird and the Crescent. The Hummingbird ran from Louisville, KY, all the way to New Orleans and back. The Crescent ran from New Orleans to Atlanta and on to Washington, D.C. and back.

Charles, John, and I sometimes sat on the bank of the ravine watching the passengers in the dining cars go by. We played games guessing where they were headed. We liked to think that somewhere out there a much bigger world was waiting to be explored.

When the war came, dozens of troop trains passed through town, sometimes stopping for water for the steam engines. We loved to wave at the soldiers who hung out the windows. They always waved back and whistled at any female who happened to be walking by. In addition to the troop trains, we also saw freight trains loaded with tanks, jeeps, armored personnel carriers, ambulances, mounted artillery pieces and other large pieces of war equipment. The trains made us feel closer to the war effort and envious of the soldiers aboard them, heading off to the war.

One day in the fall of 1943, the principal of the grammar school called us into the auditorium. He had been notified that on the following day, a special train carrying President Franklin D. Roosevelt would pass through Greenville. He had been told that the president might come out and wave to us. He urged all of us to wear our

The Trains

best dress-up clothes so we would make a good impression on the President. I remember putting on my black Sunday school knickers for the occasion.

The next morning the entire student bodies of the grammar school and high school lined up by grade. We then began the long walk, two by two, to the train station where we proudly took our places to see the "President of the United States of America," as our principal called him. Anticipation and excitement filled the air. No U.S. president had ever been in Greenville.

Standing eagerly in straight lines at the station along with the crowd of townspeople, we heard the distant train whistle announcing its approach.. In a few minutes, we could see it. As it headed towards us, we realized it was going full speed. We all raised our hands to begin waving and cheering for the President, but the train's thunderous wheels and hissing steam drowned us out. In a flash, the big locomotive and its precious cargo roared past us, leaving a thick cloud of cinders, smoke and steam in its wake. We were all covered with it. We stood there in complete silence and utter disappointment watching the train disappear down the tracks at full speed. Not a one of us saw the President, who, we were later told, was in the last car with shades drawn. There was nothing left to do but make that same long -- and now rueful -- walk back to school. All for nothing. Our only hollow claim was that we had seen the exact train car that carried President Roosevelt through Greenville. We consoled ourselves with knowing at least we had been within a few feet of the sleeping president.

After the second grade, trains took on a special meaning for me. Each summer Daddy lined up free trip passes for my brother and me. He could get one set of trip passes for each of us once a year from all of the various railroad companies. We had a wide choice of where we could travel free. He took us separately on a long trip each year loosely in conjunction with his agricultural work. He took me to New Orleans, St. Louis, Nashville, Cincinnati and Louisville. Dan got to go to San Antonio, El Paso and Mexico. He also went to Chicago and Washington. We always went to some historic site or to the zoo in each city we visited. These trips each summer led me out of Greenville to a world that I was yearning to see.

Thirteen

PROFESSOR ORVILLE G. HARDING

G reenville may have been a small town where religion, civic clubs and choice of gasoline defined a lot of people, but it also had its share of eccentrics. My father gravitated towards these people. Although he was pretty conventional himself, a number of his acquaintances had unusual ideas and odd obsessions. One was convinced the South could only be saved by switching from cattle to sheep farming. Another talked endlessly about growing wheat instead of cotton -- "crop diversity," he called it. Another was obsessed with Native American grapes. He thought the wild muscadine grape could be made into a fine, top-selling wine and got Daddy thinking that, too. Daddy actually made five gallons of muscadine wine each year, which was the legal annual limit for homemade wine or beer. He persuaded Momma, a strict teetotaler, that this was a good thing. After all, wine was mentioned frequently in the Bible. Daddy's wine was as sweet as honey. He let me taste it once and I thought it was awful.

Of all of Daddy's unusual acquaintances, Professor Orville G. Harding was a favorite, at least at first. He, his wife Nodeen, their daughter Geraldeen and son Orville Jr. became attachments to our family. At least until Momma put an end to it.

Clifton K. Meador M.D.

Prof. Harding had an unusually loud voice and a strange, affected guttural accent. I assume this came from his years as a college professor, spending long hours lecturing to large classrooms of students at Mississippi State University. He called Daddy "Doctor Meador," except it came out "DOC-ATARR MEE-DER."

The Hardings lived out in the country about 10 miles from town, totally isolated from any community. Prof. Harding had a Ph.D. in agronomy, which is best described as the study of scientific farming, soil management and crop production. At least that's what Daddy told me it meant. Harding had retired early from the faculty of Mississippi State as a professor of agronomy. His plan was to take all his scientific knowledge and apply it to his own farm. He dreamed of the ideal operation with all the newest and best practices for growing crops and raising livestock.

With Daddy's background in horticulture and animal husbandry, he was immediately attracted to Prof. Harding and his ideas. Finding a Ph.D. professor of agronomy in the midst of barely educated sharecroppers and tenant farmers was for Daddy like discovering a fine diamond in a five-and-ten-cent store. He could not wait to be a consultant for this grand idea -- a perfectly designed farm based on scientific principles and with an actual professor of agronomy to boot.

Like Prof. Harding, Daddy dreamed of a perfect model farm based on the best scientific knowledge. A farm that raised only the best cows, hogs and sheep. One where the crops were rotated perfectly to enhance the soil. A farm where only the latest experimental grasses were planted. A farm with perfect diversity of crops and livestock that could survive drought, hurricanes or disease.

But in the end, Prof. Harding's farm was as far from Daddy's dream as possible. It wasn't long before the truth was evident:

Professor Orville G. Harding

Harding was ill-equipped to execute his grand ideas. His science was sound, but his ability to apply that science in practical ways was not. The big problem came in the professor's lack of farming experience and his inability to plan. He had no idea how to do the daily details of farming. Put bluntly, the professor's ideal farm was a disaster.

Daddy was a rescuer of the first order in all things, and he could not sit idly by watching the professor's failed efforts. He tried to help salvage the experiment by suggesting basic changes in the professor's farming practices. It went like this:

"Professor, you must get some sheds over your tractors. They're rusting," Daddy would say.

..."Are you rotating your crops? Looks like you haven't done that this season."

"… It's planting time for those grasses, you know."

Daddy went on and on trying to correct dozens of fundamental mistakes. The professor always had an answer:

"Yes, DOC-ATARR," he would begin, "ah, my son Orville Junior has that on his list to do. Now, you must hear of my new seeds. Just got the latest bulletin out of Auburn. Planting for the spring. Auburn has this new hybrid grass…" Harding would inevitably have changed the subject, completely ignoring Daddy's comments. Then he would launch into long dissertations on the varieties of grasses and the types of soil and fertilizer needed for each variety, followed by what new breeds of hogs he was considering. He seemed lost in his dreams.

"Professor," my father would finally say, "That's all interesting. But man, you are about to lose your whole operation here! You've already lost most of your hogs to cholera. You don't need anything new. I hate to see you lose it all."

Clifton K. Meador M.D.

Each visit was the same. Reasoning with Prof. Harding was futile, but Daddy never gave up.

Throughout the experiment, Daddy took Momma, Dan and me on frequent excursions to visit the Harding family. We watched the decline of the farming operation up close and personal. The Great Depression deepened. The Hardings were living in poverty. Soon our visits were more about taking food and clothing to his poor children, less about the experiment. Everything was falling apart. On the front of the house, the wind blew through large, flapping holes in the porch screens and the steps had rotted out. Pieces of rusted farming equipment scattered about in the deep Johnson grass looked like dinosaurs in the fields. Weeds had over-taken most of the crooked fences. It was a mess.

Harding's children, now in their late teens, looked pale and sickly, probably from hookworms or malaria or both. Mother always took Cokes for us to drink and forbade us to drink or eat anything at the farm. Once, she saw the daughter pull up a bucket of water from the well with a myriad of worms wiggling in it, most likely mosquito larvae. The well, too shallow, sat next door to the outdoor privy, setting up the conditions to transmit hookworm infestations and who knows what other diseases.

In the summer, at least once a month on a Saturday, we heard a loud crashing noise as Prof. Harding's extra-tall truck pulled up in front of our house. The noise came when the top of the truck scraped the limbs of a tree beside the street. The bed of the truck was enclosed on all sides by these tall walls. It was one of the professor's inventions. He said it reduced the need for multiple trips, because the tall sides increased the truck's capacity. He often quoted the exact added capacity in tons. He would talk for half an hour on the benefits of his tall truck design, ignoring the fact that his farm was a complete failure. He seemed oblivious to his

Professor Orville G. Harding

failures, lost in thought. Too long at the lectern, he was incapable of executing a plan.

We knew when they arrived in the truck that the whole family was there for the entire afternoon, hanging around until supper time when Momma had to feed them. Momma dreaded their visits, and soon she insisted we stop going to the farm. "John," she told Daddy, "We just don't need to encourage them anymore. It's time to pull back."

As hard as it was for Daddy to give up on Prof. Harding and his experiment, he knew Momma was right. We eventually stopped going to visit and the family no longer showed up in town. We heard later that they moved back to Mississippi where the professor resumed teaching at the university. Judging from his experiment in farming, it was where he belonged.

Fourteen

MISS B AND MISS CAROLINE

Our next door neighbors were Miss B and her niece Miss Caroline. It was pronounced "Care-line," actually more like "Kay-er-line" with a long "i" sound to the "line." Miss B was in her 70s when I first met her, Miss Caroline in her mid 50s. Both were spinsters, never married. Most people spoke of them as "old maids."

Miss B had been sick for over 30 years, staying in bed most days reading Charles Dickens and Sir Walter Scott novels. Her vague diagnoses were never clear and seemed to change from time to time. One time she simply was "all wore out." Other times she "nearly had a nervous breakdown." Sometimes, it was "just having a bad day." Most people accepted her as in "poor health," a category represented by several other older women in town. Old Dr. Tine, the family doctor who made weekly house calls, said she was an invalid.

Miss B was always in her nightgown and bathrobe, even when Miss Caroline took her for her Sunday afternoon car ride into the country. She couldn't stay long on these rides as they seemed to wear her out. So why change clothes? Miss B liked to drive past the First Methodist Church and then ride through the Magnolia Cemetery so she could see her family's headstones. She never got out of the car.

Once a week, usually on Tuesdays after supper, Dr. Tine pulled up in his green 1936 Chevrolet to make his weekly house call. After setting his black bag on the bed, he always checked Miss B's blood pressure and pulse. Then he had her stick out her tongue before he listened to her heart through her nightgown, sighing constantly as he listened. When these rituals were completed, he took a deep breath and exhaled with a long comforting sigh, as if to say, "Well, Miss B, things are looking better."

On other visits, Dr. Tine sometimes brought along his nurse, Miss Francie. When the neighbors saw him get out of his car with Miss Francie, they assumed Miss B had made a turn for the worse, which was usually correct. Something in Miss Caroline's voice on the telephone told Miss Francie that she needed to accompany Dr. Tine on the next house call.

After his examining rituals, Dr. Tine would turn to Miss Francie and say. "Miss Francie, give Miss B 1cc of kutapressin." Then he would pause, nod his head a bit and say, "No, make it 2cc's and I better give the injection myself." Dr. Tine was uncanny in his ability to adjust the dosage of kutapressin on the spot, deciding whether he or Miss Francie would give the injection. By injecting the kutapressin himself, he was at least more than doubling the potency of the effect because doctor-injected medicine was much more potent than nurse-injected, even if the medication was as worthless as kutapression. Kutapressin was an extract of cow's liver, then thought to be an essential for good health, especially in patients like Miss B. In those days, the concept of a placebo effect had not yet been identified, but it was very much in practice. Physicians like Dr. Tine understood well the effect that "medical" rituals and attention from a caring doctor had on these so-called

Miss B And Miss Caroline

invalids. On most visits, Dr. Tine either adjusted the dosage of one of the tonics or added a new one. He reserved kutapressin for more serious relapses. Sometimes, he spoke to Miss Caroline on the way to the door. "If Miss B is not better by tomorrow, I will have Miss Francie come by and give her an enema." Everyone in those pre-antibiotic times knew the full power of an enema.

Miss Caroline had several nieces and nephews who lived out on the family farm, about 14 miles from town. When they came to town on Saturday, as did many farmers who came to visit kin, they stopped by Miss B's and Miss Caroline's to check on Miss B's "condition." In fact that was one of her diagnoses: "a condition."

Lowe Smathers, one of Miss B's nephews, was a classmate of mine in high school. When he appeared next door, I frequently would go over to visit with him and his sister. That's how I got to see and study Miss B up close. On her good days, when she sat on the screen porch, Lowe and I sometimes visited with her. It was obvious that she used many ointments and unguents. She smelled strongly of camphor and Ben-Gay.

Lowe and I enjoyed passing and kicking the football in Miss Caroline's front yard. Sometimes, Miss Caroline would stick her head out of the front door and hold her finger to her lips, signaling us to be quiet. "Shhhh, Miss B is having a sinking spell," she would caution us.

Miss Caroline hovered closely over Miss B, constantly monitoring her "condition." She let everyone visiting know how Miss B was doing in an hour-by-hour report. There were several definable stages. Miss B could be doing "just fine," meaning she could visit in the living room, go on her own to the kitchen or, in warm weather, join the crowd on the screen porch. On those days, she was the life of the party, telling stories and even leading the laughter.

Clifton K. Meador M.D.

But then just as suddenly, Miss B could start to have a "bad day." On bad days, Miss B stayed in bed all day and took her meals on a tray, served by Miss Caroline or the black maid Josephine. In between "just fine" and "bad day" were several ill-defined states, such as "having the miseries" or just feeling "wore out." On the bad days, Miss Caroline would urge us out of the house, whispering "Shhh, Miss B is having a bad day." Of course, she could make rapid turnarounds and be "just fine" by the same afternoon.

Miss B's bedroom was at the front of the house in a converted dining room that opened with French doors into the adjacent living room. From this vantage point, Miss B could review the passing scene on the street in front of the house. She could, if she chose, join visitors in the living room or she could draw the curtains on the French doors and stay in her bed. The kitchen was adjacent to her converted dining room and accessible through a swinging door, through which Josephine brought Miss B her meals on a tray. Her room was situated perfectly to adjust for maximum swings in Miss B's "condition."

Miss B was a devout Methodist but had been unable to attend church services for over a decade. Rev. Edward Pennington, the Methodist minister, came by every week to call on Miss B. He frequently reported on her condition to the congregation at the Sunday morning service, advising all to call ahead before visiting to make sure Miss B was strong enough to see visitors. Miss B's name had been on the prayer list in the church's weekly bulletin for over two decades.

I always wondered about Miss B. What strange disease could take such dramatic swings, even in the course of a day? Many years later, when I was in medical school, I asked Daddy what disease Miss B had. He said directly, "Oh, I don't think she had any specific disease. She was an invalid. You know, just a plain invalid."

Miss B And Miss Caroline

Miss B wasn't the only person clinging to a nebulous illness in those days. Invalids were all over the place, cared for by someone who believed they were seriously ill. The secondary gain of any illness is huge even if it doesn't really exist. Dr. Tine was a master in carrying Miss B along without confronting her real state of health, as he probably understood she couldn't function as a well person. Back then, doctors were masters of the bedside manner. In most cases, that was all they had to work with.

Miss B died quietly in her sleep. She was 89 years old. After that, Miss Caroline married Rayford Bucher, a bachelor lawyer whom she had been dating for more than 20 years. After the marriage, Bucher moved into Miss Caroline's house, where they lived for many more years.

Fifteen

Mamie and Boogers

When I was 11 years old, I saw a booger.

I remember it like it was yesterday. Boogers are dark scary creatures that come out at night in the winter time. At least that's what Mamie, our cook, taught me. She believed in boogers and was terrified of them. They were somehow connected to voodoo, which was still practiced in Greenville's black community in those days. From the time I was a little boy, Mamie told me all about these awful creatures. She was encyclopedic on the subject. She didn't do this to frighten me. She did it because she wanted me to beware. She believed and made a believer out of me, too.

The year I saw one was 1942, a cold, windy December night. Even though it was Alabama, the winters could be brutal. It was often a damp chill that had a way of intensifying the reading on the thermometer, especially when the wind kicked up. On this particular night, Momma had told me I could go to the movie with my friends John and Charles and walk home by myself if I got back before 9. I said I would.

Clifton K. Meador M.D.

Everything was going fine until John and Charles persuaded me to stay for the second showing of the movie. That was a big mistake on my part. Not only was that going to make me late getting home, it also meant watching for the second time that night the horrible-but-irresistible *Frankenstein*. That hideous giant monster with dangling bandages and a spike through his neck escaping from Dr. Frankenstein's castle laboratory and wandering into the village. Mobs of angry citizens with flaming torches chasing him down. A dead man made of human parts and brought to life by electricity. Everything about that movie terrified me. Now I had to walk home on a dark, cold night.

As we walked out of the picture show into a pitch dark and vacant Commerce Street, I realized it was nearly 10 p.m. I knew I was in deep trouble for being over an hour late and disobeying Momma. John, Charles and I began the quiet walk toward home down Commerce, now deadly still except for the sound of the cold wind blowing a cloud of leaves down the middle of the empty street. We were the only humans in sight. Frankenstein was behind every corner.

My house was only six blocks from the Ritz Theater, but at that moment it seemed like a mile. First, John got to his house. Then Charles dropped off at his. Now I was all alone. A combination of fears whirled in my mind: the Frankenstein monster, the black moonless night, Momma's wrath at my being late -- but most of all, the unspeakable terror of the boogers.

I began to run through the darkness with four more blocks to home. Soon I was at top speed. I could hear Mamie's voice playing over and over in my mind:

"Boogers live up in trees and up under houses. They likes it dark... only come out in winter... when it's cold and ain't nobody outside...they loves the wind...they is always after somebody. Specially if you be alone."

Mamie And Boogers

The wooden, rickety, railroad bridge loomed ahead. It had stuck in my mind since leaving the movie. I knew I had to cross it. There was no other path to take. Mamie's booger lessons played over and over.

"Only thing to keep 'em away is to whistle or talk out loud. Boogers don't like talking."

Panting for breath, I tried to whistle. No luck. So I hummed tunes as loud as I could, now running faster toward that wooden railroad bridge.

"In winter... at night... no moon... boogers come outta hiding... all over the place...up under bridges... where the wind is howling and moaning.

I could see the shadowy frame supports of the wooden bridge and the faint streetlight on the other side of it.

"Worst place under the railroad bridge..., boogers loves to swarm ... howl with the wind...more than a dozen boogers up under that bridge...don't you never go up under there."

The railroad tracks ran through the center of town in a deep ravine. The wooden bridge ran from one edge of the ravine over the tracks to the other side. If I could get across that bridge without being caught by the boogers, I would be safe under the streetlight on the other side.

"Boogers don't like light."

I now ran at full speed across the dreaded bridge. The wooden planks rattled as I stomped across them. I could hear the wind howl and moan in high pitches beneath the bridge. It had a human, desperate quality, like dead people trying to talk. A strong wind blew in my face, slowing my run. Every hair on my head and neck stood on end. Gooseflesh covered my body. My mouth felt dry. My terror was now full blown.

I got to the other side of the bridge and stopped under the last streetlight. I stood there in its glow bent over with my hands on my knees, gasping for air but temporarily safe. I now had two choices. I could continue down the street where there were two more blocks to my house with two more streetlights to protect me. Or I could make a radical decision and take a shortcut home across the unlit schoolyard. The shortcut would save me several minutes but meant crossing that sprawling stretch of darkness and the tall, gangly oak tree standing in the middle of it. I knew that huge oak tree would be filled with boogers, especially on a cold and windy moonless late December night.

Emboldened by my safe run across the bridge, I made a snap decision. I hopped down the hill into the jet-black schoolyard, running again at top speed. I felt like my legs were churning faster than they ever had in my whole life. Before I knew it, the dreaded oak tree was right in front of me, its tangled branches reaching wildly overhead. That's when I heard it -- the flapping sound of wings. I looked over my shoulder to see a huge black form swoop down toward me. Long red flames spewed from its mouth like a flying dragon, and a brilliant yellow light beamed from its eyes. Clearly, I was its prey. It hissed and spat fire in my direction, as its beating wings whipped the frigid night air around me into a fierce wind.

As to what happened next, I can't say. All consciousness ceased. My mind turned off. One moment I was passing under the massive oak tree; the next I was standing on the porch of my house. One minute I was nearly in the clutches of a flame-breathing, yellow-eyed booger; a split-second later I had somehow been transported several hundred yards to the safety of my own doorstep. Time simply jumped.

Mamie And Boogers

I flung open the door and stumbled into the living room where Daddy, Momma and Dan were gathered around the radio listening to one of the weekly shows. A gentle fire crackled in the fireplace. Frisky, warmed from lying on the hearth, jumped in my lap and licked my face.

"Well!" Momma began, looking up from her sewing with a very serious face. "You are certainly late, young man. Where have you been?"

I was trying desperately to calm my breathing and gather my thoughts into some sort of plausible response. I decided maybe she wouldn't notice what a state I was in, so I did my best imitation of non-chalance. "Oh," I began, faking it, "just walking home from the movie with John and Charles. We stayed a little while over."

"Why are you breathing so hard?" she asked.

"Oh, just decided to run part of the way."

You just didn't tell parents about seeing boogers. That was all there was to it. I flopped on the floor and stared into the coal fire in the grate, finally catching my breath. Its warmth enveloped me. I settled into the safe and protective coziness of home and family with Frisky in my lap. Suddenly, the whole booger episode seemed very far away.

In the days after, I wished I could tell Mamie about seeing that booger. She would have believed me. But by then Mamie, Billy and the rest of her family had moved away.

If I close my eyes today I can still see that flame-spewing, yellow-eyed booger coming right out of that old oak tree. And he was heading right for me.

Sixteen

The Reverend Ralph Morgan

When I was in my teens, there were three powerful inhibiting forces against having premarital sex – pregnancy, getting syphilis and fear of eternal hellfire and damnation.

Fear of getting a girl pregnant was at the top of the list. Birth control pills were more than a decade in the future. The only abortions available were criminal ones, and everyone knew they often killed the woman. Pregnancy meant mandatory marriage, no matter how undesirable the girl. Shotgun marriages were real events, and they erased forever any chance of a successful future.

Syphilis or any venereal disease was also embedded in my young mind as a social disgrace. But it was Leon who really convinced us of its horrors. Leon did not have syphilis, but he know all the details of its treatment. Annual blood testing for syphilis was mandatory for all citizens of Alabama for a brief period. If you tested positive, they hauled you off involuntarily in a rented bus for a month's stay at the Army Air Force Base in Montgomery. Every Saturday, a yellow school bus pulled up back of the post office. We called it the "Syphilis Bus." All the syphilis-positive men got on it with their hats hung low over their faces to hide from public view. We knew these men had to get 21 shots, and Leon told us the Army used a square needle to stick you in the belly. That did it. For boys about to be 15, those images were a powerful deterrent.

If fear of getting a girl pregnant or syphilis and the dreaded 21 shots with square needles in your belly weren't enough, there was always hellfire and eternal damnation. I want you to meet The Reverend Ralph Morgan.

The Reverend Ralph Morgan was minister of the Sandy Bottom Primitive Baptist Church. Sandy Bottom was in the southern end of Butler County. It was best known for its poor people, bootleggers and unproductive soil. Greenville's second whore, Maw Gooden, lived near there. There were no black people in that section of the county, because there had never been any slaves. The land was too poor to support slaves or sharecroppers. No one wanted to risk money on land that barren. One of my father's litanies was about how it's impossible to "rise above the land." I think this was inspired by Sandy Bottom.

Given the depressed educational level and low moral tone of the populace, The Reverend Ralph Morgan had plenty to occupy his time. Never was there a better combination of depravity and the right man to address it. Reverend Morgan took to his calling with a vengeance. To say he was a zealot underestimates his passion.

But unlike most ministers who gave equal time to all the deadly sins, Reverend Morgan had his mind on only one: fornication. He was the John Brown of fornication. If God, through some wild stretch of the imagination, designed a system after the U.S. justice system, Reverend Morgan would have been the attorney general of fornication.

The Reverend Ralph Morgan

My first encounter with the righteous Reverend came in high school. The Sandy Bottom Primitive Baptist Church was a member of the Butler County Ministerial Association, which is how we in Greenville came to know Reverend Morgan. Among other duties, this association supplied preachers in rotation to do the morning devotional over the school's newly installed loudspeaker system. One morning, our high school principal introduced Reverend Morgan as our speaker for the day.

Over the loudspeaker we heard him begin. "I am Reverend Morgan of the Primitive Baptist Church of Sandy Bottom. I come before you with my Bible in my hand and my head turned toward heaven. I am here to speak on one sin and one sin only. That sin is fornication. Fornication comes from lust. Lust is the most deadly of the deadly sins. Let me read what the Good Book tells us about fornication."

With that, he read something about the unrighteous not inheriting the kingdom of God. Then he continued talking about fornicators and idolaters and adulterers and about how all of those were "going to hell! *Flee fornication!!*" he began yelling into the microphone.

His tone became edgier and his volume, louder. "When you see those majorettes and cheerleaders twirling and bouncing their breasts, don't you look! Don't you let them show you those *tight little underpants*. Turn your heads away from sin and lust! Look away!! Just...look... AWAY!!"

In his fervor, he managed to point out every desirable feature of the "half-dressed girls," as he called them. He was very specific about what we should "look away" from. The more detail he laid out about "the titillating and undulating breasts and thighs that the Devil used to attract all male sinners," the more animated his voice became. And hellfire and eternal damnation awaited anyone weak enough to give in to those temptations!

The devotional got so heated and graphic that the principal finally had to shut down the microphone in the middle of Reverend Morgan's devotional, but not before we heard the two of them arguing. "Reverend, please," the principal said, "you need to tone it down...." Then the loudspeaker system was cut off.

It was the one and only time Reverend Morgan participated in the high school morning devotional, but not the only time the citizens of Greenville received a strong dose of his powerful preaching. The Butler County Ministerial Association rotated its presidency each year. In ordinary times, the position was purely honorary with small duties like saying a prayer at a football game or on the Fourth of July or some other occasion. Whenever there was a ceremony that called for a prayer, the president of the Butler County Ministerial Association showed up to pray. As luck would have it, however, the year that Reverend Morgan rotated into the presidency happened to be 1944, the year Allied forces invaded northern France at Normandy. June 6 of that year -- D-Day -- marked the largest invasion by armies in the long history of man and the world. The nation was called to prayer, and the citizens in our area all gathered at the Greenville football stadium, since we were the county seat. And, of course, leading this historic occasion would be the president of the Butler County Ministerial Association -- Reverend Ralph Morgan. This was high ground indeed for him. He had the entire town and half the county coming to say prayers for the soldiers, sailors and marines. He was to lead the prayer meeting of the largest crowd ever assembled in the history of Butler County.

The stadium was a small concrete structure built on the side of the red clay hill. We had just finished high school graduation ceremonies in late May, so the wooden platform for the graduating

The Reverend Ralph Morgan

seniors was still in place. The Quarter Million Dollar Greenville High School Black and Gold Marching Band sat on the platform looking back at the large crowd. I played second trombone, so I had a full view of the audience that night, at least 4,000 people in a stadium built for 2,000. We played *Pomp and Circumstance* since it was already well rehearsed from graduation. We repeated it at least 20 times as the crowd filed onto the concrete steps and overflowed onto the grass and clay hillsides.

When the crowd was finally in place, the dignitaries walked in procession down the steep steps and onto the wooden platform. Reverend Morgan led the way. Tall and thin with stooped shoulders, he proceeded toward us through the crowd. Except for his white shirt, everything about him looked black. Not just ordinary black. His black was dull, light absorbing. His suit was dusty black and straight cut. His tie was black string. His eyes were black. His hair was black. He wore a black hat, broad brimmed with no particular shape. His shoes were black, high top, tightly laced nearly to mid calf, firmly rooting him to shoe and shoe to ground. Reverend Ralph Morgan reflected no light. The black of Reverend Morgan trapped the light and hid it, a human black hole.

By contrast, his face was pale, but stern and grim. His hollow cheeks sank inward as though life and air were being sucked out of his face. He looked like an evil version of Abe Lincoln on one of Abe's worst photographic days, sullen and haunting.

Ostensibly, we were there that night of D-day to pray for our servicemen. Reverend Morgan did not see it quite that way. As God's appointed agent not just to talk about the sins of fornication, but to pronounce it, root it out, stamp it out and, if necessary, serve warrants of arrest, he saw this as his one great opportunity. He was going to remove the sin of fornication from Greenville and Butler County once and for all. He was going to preach it out.

Clifton K. Meador M.D.

My father, who figured Reverend Morgan was going to take on the town, couldn't wait. He knew it was going to be a show. He wasn't wrong. After the head of the American Legion said a few words, followed by the congressman, the mayor and some other important people, The Reverend Ralph Morgan rose, his Bible in hand held high before the crowd.

"This book is from whence I draw my words." he began. He said something about prayers for "the soldier boys in that foreign land." Amen. Then, with no further regard to the perils of war and the brave men fighting for our freedoms, he plunged right into fornication and lust. "You know who I am talking about!" he said. "You women who taunt men with those low-cut dresses. I've seen you in town swishing up and down Commerce, half naked. It's no wonder the men give it all up and give into your wicked ways. I say to the men, look away… look away! Ignore those thighs and cleavages. DO NOT let your mind go there!"

Then he began to rail against who was in that country club, out there on the edge of town, out there close to the whores and the whoremongers and the wicked. He drew vivid imaginary pictures of what went on out there every Saturday night with the whiskey and the drunkenness and the lust and the fornication. Then, as my father had predicted, he began to point his bony finger at individuals in the crowd, saying, "You and you and you. You know who I'm talking about. Don't try to hide! You who live in Sodom and Gomorrah. You know who I mean!"

He got the Ford car dealer and the Chevrolet dealer right off. He pointed at one of the cotton gin owners who was Presbyterian and then one of the lawyers. Then he started in on the whole town -- Presbyterian, Baptist, Methodist, Gulf, Sinclair and Shell. He played no favorites and spared no civic club -- Lions, Rotarians and Kiwanis. With each jab of his finger, he spoke directly to someone in the audience, exhorting him or her to give up sinful ways and if not, promising a life of eternal hellfire and damnation.

He went on at length, "I ain't gon' call you by name. You know who you are. You who know no bounds on your lust! You who have incurable carnal incontinence! You had better listen and repent!"

There was no escape. Every person he pointed at turned red and lowered their head. Some turned to leave but thought better of it. He went on with this tirade for what seemed forever. And then he prayed for another small eternity, asking for direct intervention for all the fornicators who sat there that night while our soldier boys were away from home on those beaches in Normandy.

Amen and amen.

For weeks afterward, many of the men in town stayed angry. Reverend Morgan's D-Day debacle filled every conversation in the barbershop. Some mumbled about suing him for libel. Nobody did. After a while, the subject faded into the background. Reverend Morgan's association presidency would be over soon enough and he would be back in Sandy Bottom, but the Allied troops were finally marching toward Berlin and the end of the war. Our full attention was recaptured by news from overseas.

Seventeen

SLOOP

In sizing the town, I mentioned there was only one taxi. Sloop, the owner and driver, knew everyone in town and everyone knew him. Most of the time he parked his taxi on the street in front of the pool hall and the Waller Hotel across from the railroad station. His car was a 1933 four-door Ford with "Taxi" written with long strips of white adhesive tape on the front doors. In white paint below that was the phone number "297-W." Sloop had worked out a deal with the Waller Hotel to answer his phone calls. If somebody rang, the hotel clerk would yell out the front door for Sloop to come to the phone. He was usually behind the wheel asleep.

There was almost no taxi business from the incoming trains and buses. Traveling salesmen arriving by train could easily walk to the hotel. Friends and family coming in were usually picked up by other friends or family. But in spite of the lack of prospects, Sloop always met the two incoming buses from Mobile just in case. He also met No. 1 train from Montgomery to the north at 1 p.m. and No. 4 coming from Mobile to the south at 4 p.m.

Clifton K. Meador M.D.

To understand how Sloop made a living with his taxi, you need to understand the ramifications of Butler County being a dry county – no alcohol of any sort could be sold there. None. Every few years, somebody raised the issue of getting legal drinking onto a referendum for a public vote. But every time that happened, two forces rose up to oppose it: the bootleggers and the churches. The saying was that the bootleggers went down one side of the street while the church ministers went down the other. This unlikely coalition managed to keep Butler County and Greenville dry.

At that time, there were only 11 counties in the whole state of Alabama that could sell beer or whiskey. The state actually owned and operated all the liquor stores in those counties. Lowndes County was the wet county closest to Greenville. Fort Deposit, 12 miles to the north, was its county seat. Sloop made the 24-mile round trip several times a day, hauling whiskey to Greenville's citizens and mostly to the Waller Hotel and the traveling salesmen. Most of Sloop's income came from that.

Growing up, alcohol simply wasn't around. I don't recall ever going to a teenage party where anyone served or allowed alcohol of any sort.

Daddy was a near teetotaler under orders from Momma. As I said earlier, he made five gallons of scuppernong wine each year, the legal limit, after he had persuaded Momma that wine was OK since it was mentioned frequently in the Bible. Momma reluctantly gave in.

But Daddy's teetotaling didn't keep him from studying the drinking habits of others in town. Somehow he knew every drinker in Greenville. He came up with several interesting observations. One was that you could figure out where big drinkers lived by observing how often Sloop's taxi was parked outside their house. Another was that you could tell the amount of drinking in a house

Sloop

by the amount of outdoor furniture in the yard. None of the houses in those days were air conditioned, so getting outside was the main method for cooling off. It's a fact that drinking alcohol makes people feel warmer, which would require they spend even more time outside -- hence, Daddy's deduction. From biking around town, I think his observation was accurate.

In addition to running whiskey, the other primary source of Sloop's taxi business came from driving the traveling salesmen to and from one of the two whores in town. Louise and her daughter Pearl, as you know, lived north of town and Maw Gooden lived south. Louise had the majority of business. Bill Waller, whose father owned the Waller Hotel, was an acquaintance of mine from school and a close observer of Sloop's comings and goings. Bill watched and made mental notes of which salesmen chose which whore. He estimated Louise was 10 to 1 over Maw. Maw was more of a redneck whore than Louise, who better suited the tastes of the suited traveling salesmen who stayed at the hotel.

Sloop was a strange-looking man, tall and extremely thin with sparse black hair. His nose caved in at the bridge resembling a small saddle. His teeth were notched and separated, and he couldn't hear very well. We sensed there was something wrong with Sloop, but we didn't know what until John happened to talk to his distant cousin who was one of the town's doctors. He told John that Sloop had been born with syphilis – congenital syphilis, it was called. Not only was Sloop born with syphilis but he had developed a double rupture in his groin. Several men in town were said to have double ruptures. The term struck pure terror in all us teenage boys. We never could get an accurate description of what exactly a double rupture was, but it sounded like some sort of explosion of the genitals. None of the men ever worked again after double ruptures. People said it resulted from lifting something heavy the wrong way. From that time on, we were terrified of lifting anything.

The combination of Sloop's odd appearance, congenital syphilis and double rupture made him someone we avoided. He generated a kind of terror and wonder in all of us. There was, right or wrong, an aura of low-grade evil about him that made him untouchable. Getting syphilis from sex was bad enough, but here was someone born with the disease. We wondered if he might somehow pass on either problem if you touched him.

We kept our distance.

Eighteen

QUAIL HUNTING WITH MY FATHER

Among my fondest memories growing up were those that involved quail hunting. Not only did I love everything about the hunt itself, the time spent in the car driving to and from the field with my father, my brother or friend John produced some of the most memorable moments of my youth, funny and otherwise.

Quail hunting gave me my first -- and last -- father-to-son talk on sex education. They didn't call it "sex education" in those days, of course. The term wasn't invented. On this particular trip, my friend John had come along. This was about three years after Leon and Pearl's infamous cloakroom exhibition. By now, our libido was fully hatched and nearly full grown. John and I had both kissed girls a few months before during a spin-the-bottle game at a chaperoned party. In that fleeting moment, like being hit by lightning, we had been forever transformed from neutered boys into heterosexual males. It was that definite and irreversible, that mind-boggling and sudden. One moment we had no interest in girls, disliked them even, and the next moment girls were almost all we thought about. A few weeks later I kissed Isabel and fell in love. One Saturday at Planter's Mercantile, Roosevelt summed it up perfectly. "Boy," he said, "if you ain't thinkin' 'bout girls, yo' mind is wanderin'."

Clifton K. Meador M.D.

Whenever my father drove, he talked. He talked on many subjects, usually about what he was reading. I always thought that when he read something, he had some deep compulsion to tell somebody -- anybody -- what he had just read. He could also discuss almost any subject related to animals or plants. Especially when we were on car trips, he would set into a rambling discourse. He could move effortlessly from the details of building a trap to catch buzzards to raising Himalayan quail to shearing sheep to dipping cows for ticks to grafting camellias to stories about veterinary school at Cornell in 1906 to dissecting horses in the anatomy lab to judging cows, horses, sheep, dogs and cats. He could list and describe all of the varieties and characteristics of Native American grapes like Muscadine, locally called "scuppernongs." He had been battalion veterinary surgeon for a thousand mules with a U.S. Army ordinance division in World War I and told many stories about those experiences. His list of topics was inexhaustible.

While he was a great talker during these trips, my father was the worst driver I have ever known. When I was growing up, all our cars had dents in every fender from his repeated collisions. One of his worst habits was to back up too fast and hit something serious like a fire hydrant or light pole. Then, as if fast-forward speed would somehow undo the backward damage, he would gun the motor full throttle, throw it into first gear and then jerk the car forward, sometimes hitting whatever was in front, like a parked car. One time I remember him knocking out a rear light on the back up and a headlight on the forward lunge.

Other times on road trips, he would get so lost in his talking that he would let the car slow down to less than 10 miles an hour. Being a manual shift in those days, it would begin to lurch and stall in high gear. My brother and I would start laughing, which would ignite my father's temper, which would trigger his riding

Quail Hunting With My Father

the clutch, gunning the engine in high gear and slowly urging the car back up to highway speed. All this without missing a sentence on whatever he was talking about.

If we mentioned his poor driving, he would mumble, "Yeah, yeah I know." He never did get the hang of modern three-geared cars. I asked him why he had such trouble with them and he said something about the first cars having some sort of gear that you pumped up and down and that the new gearing confounded him.

But back to quail hunting and sex ed. So John and I were in the back seat on this particular trip and Daddy was going on strong about the best seeds to plant in a field to attract quail. He knew the seed names and was into one of his grass-and-seed litanies --fescue, lespedeza and kaley peas. He even knew the experimental seeds like API No. 2637. Right in the middle of quail feed and with no warning, he turned to John and me sitting in the back seat and said, "Better be careful. Don't go getting those girls pregnant."

Well, needless to say, I was not prepared for what I had just heard. I knew my father could be abrupt and say almost anything on his mind, a trait that likely came from growing up on a farm and his education and experiences with treating animals. He could be insensitive as to what, when and where he chose to talk about almost any subject. His favorite along these lines was to discuss the nutritional power of eggs at a meal. Frequently, when Momma served him eggs, he would go off into one of his lectures on the power of eggs. "Eggs," he would say, "have got to be the most powerful of all foods. Just imagine that one egg can generate a whole chicken -- beak, eyes, feet, guts and feathers." At which point Momma would intervene, "John, please. We are eating." It never stopped him. He would go on in detail, laying out the specific chicken parts that come from an egg.

So when he turned to John and me with advice on sex, I was not completely surprised. But I was still somewhat stunned. I don't remember what we said, but I do remember feeling my face flush. And that was it. Without missing a beat, he turned back around and resumed talking about quail feed.

He never mentioned the subject to me again. That was the only parental sex education I ever received. I got an earful from Roosevelt working at Planter's Mercantile some years later, as you will learn. But that's another story.

Also related to quail hunting was the time Daddy took my brother Dan and me out for instructions on gun safety. Daddy loved to give us instructions. Dan had turned 15 and was therefore eligible, according to Daddy's rules, to shoot a shotgun. I got to go along and observe. On the way, I sat in the front seat beside Daddy. Dan was in the back seat on the driver's side, holding Daddy's shotgun, a Browning Sweet 16. This was a 16-gauge shotgun that held five shells, but you could only load three for bird hunts. That was the legal limit.

All during the drive, Daddy was going on and on about gun safety, all the obvious stuff about not pointing the gun at people, always having the safety on, not going around with your finger on the trigger. Then his voice became especially serious. "And never, ever under any circumstances should you have a loaded gun in a car," Daddy said. Then he repeated the entire sentence, word for word, for emphasis.

Just as he said this, I heard a click in the back seat. I turned around and could not believe my eyes: Dan had loaded a shell into the gun. Daddy obviously didn't hear it and went on again about the perils of loaded guns. Then I heard *another* click and there was Dan loading a second and then a third shell into the gun, right in

Quail Hunting With My Father

Daddy's car as he was telling us not to do that. Daddy, not hearing a thing, went on talking and talking. I didn't dare say a word.

Soon we pulled into the field where Daddy was going to teach Dan how to shoot. Daddy got out of the driver's seat just as Dan emerged from the back seat, gun in hand. Then all of a sudden, *BOOM!!* The moment Dan stepped out, that gun went off into the ground narrowly missing Daddy's feet. Just as Daddy was beginning to yell, the gun went off into the ground a second time. By then Daddy was berserk, *"Good God A' mighty!! What in the hell are you doing!?! Didn't you hear a word I said? In the name of common decency. I can't believe this. You could have killed us both!!"* And on and on and on. Dan didn't say a word. We piled right back in our old Chevrolet and headed straight back into town. Daddy carried on all the way home, repeating himself over and over. The gun lesson ended before it started.

I never knew what was going on in Dan's mind when he loaded that gun at the very moment Daddy was telling him not to. The teen years are a puzzling phase of life.

When I was old enough to hunt -- and Dan had learned his safety lessons -- quail hunting with the dogs was my favorite. Daddy loved it, too. He always kept hunting dogs -- pointers. On our way to the field, the dogs rode in the trunk of the car. All Daddy would have to do was raise the lid of the trunk and those two dogs would jump right in. A brief growling fight always ensued, then they settled down on the accumulation of stuff, mostly old croaker sacks and car parts. With a piece of wood and a rope, we tied the trunk lid to let in air. Then off we would go, chugging and lurching in third gear until we finally got up some speed. Occasionally, Daddy would start off correctly in first gear and then slip past second into third gear. But even then, he usually didn't have enough speed to make the transition smoothly, so the car would buck in third until we got up to around 40 miles per hour. Of course, all this lurching and chugging wreaked havoc on his passengers, but it never phased my father. He didn't even notice.

Once at the field, the dogs jumped out of the trunk, peed and immediately began running in circles, noses to the ground. Daddy would call out "find!" or "hunt!" and off they would go. There is no sight quite like two dogs hunting out a field together, one to the right and the other to the left, crisscrossing the field and then hunting the edges. If they didn't find any birds in a few minutes, they would stop and look back for instructions. Daddy would either wave them to go right or go left or come back.

And then it would happen. Suddenly. Remarkably. One of the dogs would stop...stiffen... nose straight ahead...tail straight out... sometimes a front leg raised...still...rigid...quivering. Like a tonic seizure. There is pure magic in seeing a dog on point. Then Daddy would call, "Birds, birds, hold...hold... hold," and we would start the slow walk up to the dogs. The second dog now would also be in point, not moving, eyes glazed over, looking nowhere, as if mesmerized by the point of the first dog.

As we walked towards the dogs, we calculated every step. Cautious. A foot misplaced could snap the smallest stick, spooking the covey of quail to flush. Moving slowly, one foot at a time, waiting, guns raised to ready position, safety off, finger on the trigger. It was predetermined that I would shoot right. John would shoot left. My father had rehearsed that with us many times.

And then, after what seemed like eons, the covey would flush. I was never ready for it, that explosion of noise, feathers and birds rising, some going left, some going right, some coming straight at you and over you and the rrrrrrrrooooommmmmm sound of a covey of quail so loud and so close. You can't believe a few birds can make that much noise and fuss. You knew it would happen, yet

Quail Hunting With My Father

you were never fully ready for it. No matter how many times you hunt, you never are quite prepared for the covey rise.

The magnitude of that moment always made my heart pound and my adrenalin rush to full alert. In the midst of all the commotion, you're lucky to get off one good shot, maybe two. If you're really good, three shots. From that, you might take home one or two birds, but only the experts bag three. I once got two birds on the rise and only saw my father get three on one occasion.

After all the excitement, Daddy would call to the dogs, "Fetch! Come!" then, "Good dog, good dog," as they dropped each bird gently at his feet. We would start to hunt down the singles if the hunting had been slow and we had only found one covey of birds. If the hunting had been good and there were multiple coveys to find, we would move on to another covey and let the singles go.

Quail hunting was a winter event. The days were January cold and short. As the sun started to sink low in the sky, smoke would rise out of the farmhouses and settle over the fields. You smelled it long before you saw it. We would start to think of home and supper. Daddy called in the dogs and they jumped in the trunk, tired and happy as we headed home. If we were a long way out in the country and the car heater was blasting, I would curl up on the back seat for a nap. I could feel the intense heat of my cheeks as they warmed from the frigid, late afternoon air. Whoever had come along -- Dan or John -- would also fall asleep in the front seat. Daddy's continuous talking faded in and out as I drifted off, dreaming about supper of fricasseed quail, thick brown gravy, grits and biscuits.

Nineteen

RUBY

After Mamie moved to Detroit with her family, Momma hired Ruby as our cook and maid. Ruby cooked breakfast, dinner (the noon meal) and set out leftovers for supper. Like Mamie, she had "toting" privileges, which allowed her to "tote" food at the end of each day to feed her family. This was the Great Depression and there was so little money that food itself became a way of paying wages. As I said, my father got down to making just $85 dollars a month at the bottom of the Depression in the early 1930s.

If Mamie was into boogers and the details of their terrors, then Ruby was equally into haints and other even scarier visions. I had seen a booger, but knew little about haints. Haints, as Ruby told me, are different from boogers. Boogers come out in the winter on cold windy nights. They love dark places like under railroad bridges, under houses, up in attics and in large trees. Boogers disappear in the summer with its long days of sunlight.

In contrast, haints live only in cemeteries, down deep in graves. Haints love to jump out from behind tombstones and scare boys and girls. They can climb in and out of graves with no trouble.

Clifton K. Meador M.D.

Like boogers, they too come out only at night. They prefer moonless nights. Haints are actually the ghosts of dead people. Boogers have no human identity, but are just horrible amorphous forms of terror and evil.

Just after my 12th birthday in 1943, Ruby started working for the family. That's when she took me on as her apprentice in the world of haints and other mysteries. She told me she believed in voodoo and black magic, whatever those were. She could talk for hours about the haints she had seen.

Ruby also knew Evalina, a strange, insane and scary black woman who lived homeless on the streets of Greenville. Ruby said Evalina had evil powers. Most people just thought she was crazy. Every boy and girl in town was terrified of Evalina. Evalina (pronounced ev-er-line-ah) scavenged out of garbage cans around town. She put everything into one large cardboard box that she dragged by a rope behind her. She also had a long cloth bag used for cotton picking that she dragged behind her as she went from one garbage can to the next.

At night she lived in a lean-to shack on a dirt road out back of the Methodist Church. The roadbed of the alley was deepened by years of wagon and car traffic, forming a kind of small gully where Evalina stayed at night with her boxes and bags.

The old Magnolia cemetery, now full and abandoned, was directly across the main road from Evalina's night home. We knew the cemetery to be haunted and full of haints, according to Ruby. But, unfortunately, you couldn't get to or from the downtown picture show without passing between the cemetery and the dirt alley where Evalina lived at night.

Late one afternoon, John and I headed back down South Park Street to my house. We had gone to the Saturday movies to see the usual triple-header: a B-class movie, a cowboy movie and the

Ruby

weekly episode of the *Tarzan, The Ape Man* serial. By the time it was over, the late December sun had set. We faced Evalina's alley in the dark.

When we passed Evalina's alley, we were already running. She jumped out in front of us, laughing maniacally from deep in her throat. Between cackles, she kept yelling, "Gon' get you! Gon' get you!" followed by a wide, toothless grin.

We screamed and crossed the street to avoid her. Now we were dangerously close to the dark cemetery. I was certain we would run head-on into haints. In fact, I thought I heard them moaning, but wouldn't -- couldn't -- look. Between their ghoulish sound and Evalina's insane laugh, I was goosebumps head to toe. Our only hope was to get to the lights on my front porch.

John and I never stayed late for another Saturday movie.

Between my earlier years with Mamie's boogers and my later years with Ruby's haints, I lived my early years in dread of the dark. Those fears lasted a long time.

Looking back, I realize that much of what Mamie and Ruby taught me were superstitions of the voodoo black culture. However, there is one real episode with Ruby that remains vivid in my memory. After 70 years, I have not been able to dismiss it or explain it in terms of ordinary reality.

I need to give you some background. Momma had been sick with colon cancer for over a year. I was approaching my 14th birthday. World War II would soon be over in August of 1945. Momma was terminal and in and out of a confused consciousness.

One night, I heard Ruby scream. She continued to scream hysterically as I ran to the living room where she had fallen to the floor. She sat up and pointed to the screen door on the front of the house.

"Hit's the death moth. Lord God... Sweet Jesus... He done sent the death moth for yo dear mother. Jesus done sent the death moth." Ruby was sobbing and ringing her hands. "Yo Momma gonna die."

I went to the screen door. There it was -- a huge, iridescent green insect, a moth. The green appeared to be pulsating as if lit by some weak internal light source. Both the body and the wings were more than six inches long. The wings moved very slightly, so I knew it was alive. Every hair on my neck stood up. My breathing increased. I could feel my heart pounding in my chest. I stared and stared. I had never seen anything like that, nor have I since. It was the largest insect I would ever encounter.

I flicked the screen on the door and the moth flew away into the night.

My mother died a week later.

Over the years, I have told this story to many friends and acquaintances. No one I know had seen or even heard of a death moth. I even began to doubt my own memory until I found this on the internet:

Death, Omen of Death

Death is symbolized by many aspects of Lepidoptera. In Maryland, if a white butterfly enters your house and flies around you, it foretells death. In some parts of the country, if a moth lands on the mother of a newborn child, that child will soon die. Italian-Americans view the appearance of a moth in their home as a sign of the impending death of someone they know.

Ruby

There is a moth in Europe called the Death's Head Sphinx Moth. It represents death to many Europeans because of the clear outline of a skull on its back. Salvador Dali made use of this symbol in an interpretation of a Currier and Ives print, "The Life of a Fireman."

There are numerous other examples of Lepidoptera symbolizing death. It is said if a caterpillar measures your entire length or girth you will die. Samoans felt if they captured a butterfly it meant they would be struck dead. In Brunswick, if the first butterfly spotted in spring is a white one, it was an omen of death. The Celts believed that seeing a butterfly flying at night meant death. The chrysalis or pupal stage symbolizes death in Christian art.

At least there is confirmation that others across time and geography have seen and believed moths to be omens of death. I don't think of myself as superstitious, but seeing that moth and the timing of my mother's death still puzzle me. Are there really omens in this world? Is there some other reality? What else did Ruby know but not share? I have no answers to these questions.

I could never get Ruby to tell me how she learned about the Death Moth or where she heard about such things. She refused to talk about it. Every time I raised the question, she would get nervous, shake her head and just walk away.

Twenty

Buzzard Hunting

I am not sure who came up with the idea of buzzard hunting, but I think it was Leon. He found this buzzard roost and that led to the idea of hunting. We were halfway through our senior year of high school.

Leon lived out near Monterey, a tiny crossroads village in the country. On his way to and from town in his pickup, he passed a pen where they slaughtered cattle. The slaughter pen was designed to kill and dress out beef for the local meat market. It had several enclosed areas for the cattle and long chutes made from wooden fencing. The men would lead the cattle down the narrow passages, where they would trap the animals motionless between the sides of the fences and shoot them in the head. Then they pulled the carcass out of the side of the chute onto a platform-like table. There they skinned and divided it into various cuts of meat for sale to local markets. Leon had watched the whole process and described it in gruesome detail to Charles, John and me.

The pens and slaughter areas were filled with tall pines and oaks. That's where the buzzards perched on tree limbs waiting to eat entrails and odd pieces of meat on the ground left over from the slaughter. We didn't realize it, but the owner of the slaughter pens had a nifty, free garbage disposal system thanks to the birds. It never occurred to us that anyone would get upset if we shot a few of them. We actually thought we were helping him clean up the place.

Leon parked his pickup truck in my driveway on this particular day, since my home was barely 100 yards from the high school. Basketball season was over, which meant we had nothing to do in the afternoons. We had mapped out an adventure. We were going buzzard hunting.

Charles, John, Leon and I raced to my house. We grabbed our shotguns from the back of my garage, jumped in Leon's truck and sped towards the slaughter pens and the buzzard roost. Leon didn't have a shotgun, so John let him use one of his extras.

From over a mile away, we could see buzzards circling high in the sky, attracted by the odors of death. As we got closer the pens appeared, and above them all these huge black birds huddled in the trees. Seeing more than a dozen buzzards sitting and waiting patiently for food was an eerie experience, like some grisly death scene from a Frankenstein movie.

We had to wait until the slaughter workers left before we could do any hunting. Somewhere in the back of our minds, I think we believed we were on a mission of mercy. We didn't like the idea of slaughtering cows the way they were doing it, so if we killed all the buzzards they would have to stop the slaughter. Something naive like that. However, that's not at all the way it worked. As we would soon find out.

That first day of hunting, we were surprised when not a single buzzard fell despite a barrage of shots from our guns. All we heard

Buzzard Hunting

were loud flapping sounds as the flock -- or "wake," as a group of buzzards is called --flew away.

Charles figured it out. "There's no wonder," he said. "We all got birdshot. We need buckshot if we're going to kill any buzzards."

He was right. Birdshot is a very small pellet used to shoot quail or doves. The shell sends out a cloud of these tiny pellets that kill small birds at a short distance. Birdshot only made big buzzards fly away angry.

The next day we loaded buckshot shells. Our goal was to shoot as many buzzards as we could before they flew away. In order not to spook them, we decided we needed to all shoot at once. On the count of three, all of us shot into the trees. Eight to 10 dead buzzards plummeted to the ground. It was a spectacular sight. Their sheer size amazed me. They probably weighed 20 or more pounds.

We each got two buzzards that day. Buoyed by our success and the notion of crippling the awful slaughter operation, we went back the next day. And the next. Every afternoon after school, we rushed to my house, got our shotguns, loaded into the truck and drove to the slaughter pen buzzard roost. It was a contest to see who could shoot the most buzzards before they all flew away. Leon was the best shot and usually won. He got two birds each day.

We had been buzzard hunting every day for a week before we ran into trouble. On the last day, as we got out of Leon's truck and walked up underneath the roost, we heard voices. Their volume escalated into yelling, followed by a barrage of shotgun blasts. "You little sons of bitches!" someone hollered, "Get out of here! I ain't gonna have no one shooting my buzzards!!"

With that, a man in overalls fired two more shots, still yelling. We could hear the shotgun pellets hitting the roof of Leon's truck.

Some stung us as we started to run. Then we saw two more men come out onto the road and level their shotguns at us. Two more shots fired from about 70 yards peppered our necks, legs and backs. We heard more shot raining down on Leon's truck. Terrified, three of us leaped into the back of the pickup and buried down flat, while Leon jumped into the driver's seat, fired it up and gunned it into a full spin before speeding off toward town. We barely escaped getting shot again.

Thankfully, their shotguns were loaded with birdshot. We would have been seriously injured -- or worse -- had it been buckshot. We were still lucky that none of the small shot caused any injury. The men had definitely made their point. Our buzzard hunting days were over.

But not for Leon. He kept the caper alive during recess in his usual fashion, embellishing the details of our daring and almost deadly hunts. We heard it over and over and over.

Twenty One

JOHN CHARLES ROBERTS

L ife in a small town in the Deep South in the 1930s and '40s was both isolated and restricted. Aside from the unbridgeable gulf between blacks and whites, there was an ethnic homogeneity among the native whites. Few outsiders had come to settle here during the past 50 years – one family of Italians, one Jew (whose wife and daughter remained in New York), one World War I war bride from France who spoke in a thick French accent and one family of 13 Catholics who emigrated from Ireland. When taking stock of our ethnic community, some people added, "Oh yes, and there are three Republicans." When my family moved to town in 1936, even we were looked on as strangers for a few years.

At age 6, I saw my first Yankee. The principal of our grammar school stood on stage at assembly and introduced Frankie who had just moved to town from "way up north." He told us to be nice to Frankie, "even if he is a Yankee." The principal wasn't joking. I recall thinking how surprised I was that Frankie looked like the rest of us. I had expected something very different from hearing my Uncle Cedric bad-mouth Yankees. He viewed the South as a previously occupied and subjugated nation. He never got past the Civil War.

Clifton K. Meador M.D.

It was the similarity of everyone in Greenville that made John Charles Roberts stand out so vividly. His father had been probate judge and he had grown up in the town. John Charles had come from within, arisen from the town, grown on the same soil -- and yet there he was. Like some occasional plant that develops quite differently from all the surrounding ones.

I first saw John Charles at Mrs. Riley's Boarding House. After my mother died, my father and I ate there every Sunday after church in the fall of 1945. A full plate and all you could eat cost 50 cents. Since the boarding house was a short walk from the First Baptist Church, by the time we got there the group for the second sitting was about to go into the dining room. The Methodists and Presbyterians always got there for first sitting because their preachers finished preaching on time. Methodists and Presbyterians either didn't like long-winded ministers or they got hungry earlier on Sundays. Baptist preachers always went over time.

I don't believe John Charles belonged to any church. He just showed up for Sunday dinner. "Dinner" was what we called the noon meal, even during the week. The night meal was supper.

These Sunday dinners gave me my first up-close look at John Charles. He was sitting with his legs crossed, the right leg draped and hanging loosely over the left knee. This position pulled up his trousers at the ankle exposing silk stockings and black ballerina shoes. I remember the shock when I saw the stockings and slippers. I couldn't wait to tell my father, but I couldn't say anything because the room was full of people.

John Charles Roberts came from an old and respected family. The Roberts had been early settlers and later successful business and professional people. John Charles's father, before his death, had been well known and liked. John Charles was Judge Roberts's only child, born when the judge was in his 50s. Even at an early

116

John Charles Roberts

age, John Charles was not like the other boys in town. The judge removed him from the public school because children teased him severely. He then had his boy tutored at home in the family mansion just off Commerce Street.

The judge was determined to build a life for John Charles, sometimes by strange means. At one time, the judge erected a wooden fence in the backyard and had John Charles throw bricks from one side of the wall to the other, back and forth. Nobody knew the purpose for this odd activity. Some said it was a form of punishment. Some said it was something the judge devised to keep John Charles busy and out of trouble. Some thought it was a device to build up John Charles's muscles so he would look less feminine. Someone said they heard the judge say he built the fence so John Charles could learn to do something, even if it was just throwing bricks. Some theorized that it was the unusual exercise itself that caused John Charles to grow up to be strange.

As the years went on, the judge and his wife and John Charles sequestered themselves in the large house and gradually withdrew from the life of the town. First the judge died. Then John Charles left town to places unknown. Who could blame him? No one had seen John Charles for many years until his mother died and he returned to Greenville. That was just a few weeks before I first saw him at Mrs. Riley's boarding house.

As he perched there on the chair waiting for his turn at the table, John Charles held onto one knee with both hands. As he spoke. he exaggerated every gesture and facial expression with great drama. In a moment, John Charles had launched into a soliloquy worthy of the stage.

"I just *wish* you could have seen those despicable women!" he began. "They had *the nerve* to come calling on me. All those years they turned their backs on my sweet mother and now -- NOW -- they come up on my porch with those dreadful, tacky flowers?!? I told them what I thought. I told them what I was going to do with their flowers. I told them I was going to put those flowers in the middle of the street so the horses and mules and wagons could run over them!!"

By this time, he was quite agitated, talking fast with side-to-side movements of his head and fluttering eyelids. He had a way of shutting his eyes, turning his head to one side and tilting his chin into the air when he was most upset. It was as if this would shut out the world. As I watched his performance with great fascination, I noticed traces of lipstick and rouge.

Each Sunday for several weeks, John Charles showed up at the boarding house. And each Sunday he held center attention, still upset with the women of the town. He accused them of coming to see him out of curiosity, not out of concern for his dear departed mother.

Then one week he didn't show up. We heard he had enrolled at the University of Alabama. Later, we heard he moved to Mexico.

The next time John Charles crossed my path was about a year later. In fact, he had gone to Mexico and hooked up with a young Mexican man. But the couple had now moved back into the family mansion just off Commerce Street and opened an antique shop in the downstairs of the house. You can imagine the stir this caused in our small Southern town in the 1940s. The talk at Mrs. Riley's boarding house on Sundays was saturated with it.

Not long after John Charles moved back, word had it that one day he went into the post office and demanded to see the postmaster. When the postmaster came to the window, John Charles slammed down a stack of magazines and letters on the counter. He told the postmaster that he was no longer "John Charles Roberts" and that he would refuse to accept any more mail by that name. He was now to be called "Juan Carlos Roberto," and any mail not so addressed would be immediately returned to the post office. With that, he whirled around and swished his way out onto the street. Of course, word spread quickly down Commerce Street. The people couldn't wait to call John Charles by his new name. Within days, he became "Juan Carlos."

Once a week, always on Saturday, Juan Carlos slung a duffle bag of dirty clothes over his shoulder and headed down past the Ritz Theater toward Sunshine Cleaners. Juan Carlos lived just around the corner from Commerce Street where the Ritz was located. Whenever the movie ended, a crowd of teenagers spilled out into the Street. It was a favorite gathering spot, and taunting Juan Carlos was a favorite sport.

Whenever Juan Carlos came sashaying through the crowd of teenagers, the whistles and catcalls would start. "Haaay Juan Carlos," someone would yell. "Where's your boyfriend?" The remarks got more and more ugly and abusive. Juan Carlos held his head up high and kept walking, ignoring it all. Some thought he actually enjoyed the audience and timed his walk accordingly.

Juan Carlos continued to bring incorrectly addressed mail back into the post office, slam it down on the counter and walk away in a huff. He kept our small community entertained, but the town kept its distance. Homosexuality in those days was seen as deviancy and buried, suppressed, denied. One of the school principals had been run out of town a few years before only on suspicion he might be gay. There was never any proof. Besides Juan Carlos and his partner, Greenville had two other known homosexuals. Both were predatory pedophiles. In those days, they weren't tried and convicted in a proper court of law. Instead, they were periodically beaten up by the high school football players and shunned. As for lesbians, they were neither in our vocabulary nor wildest imaginations back then, even though there were several female teachers living together as couples.

All this is to say that Juan Carlos and his boyfriend were a source of great curiosity for us in our closed-minded small town. Given that and the fact there was so little to do for excitement, one night John and I decided to sneak up on the large house to spy on Juan Carlos and his boyfriend. We couldn't imagine what two men living together did, especially given that one was Mexican and the other was some sort of weird cross-dressing homosexual.

We parked our bikes off to one side of the sprawling lawn and stooped down beneath the bushes. Then we half-crawled our way to the edge of the grand porch at the front of the house. We saw our tactics as a dash across no man's land in some battle ground assault, still caught in our war fantasies.

Lights were on in the large living room, shining out through the windows onto the wide front porch. As we raised up ever so cautiously to peek over the windowsills, we could see one figure dash across the room, then another. After a few minutes watching this curious movement, it came to us: *"They're dancing!"* We could hear a phonograph record playing some fast Spanish tango as the two men strutted back and forth across the room. They paused occasionally to toast each other with wine glasses.

It is difficult to convey the strangeness and surrealism of the scene that played out as two small-town, completely naïve boys stared in disbelief. We were dumbfounded. Nothing in our small worlds had prepared us for what we were witnessing.

About that time, John bumped into a large vase on the porch. It tumbled to its side and rolled against the window. The music stopped, as did our hearts. Before we could scramble out of there, the front door flew open. There stood Juan Carlos dressed head to toe in a costume that looked vaguely Arabian. I think I had seen something like it at the movies once.

"Who's there?!" he called out. "We heard you! Come out this instant!"

At that, John and I took off across the lawn, jumped on our bikes and pedaled down the street as fast as we could go. We were terrified, but we had escaped. Juan Carlos hadn't recognized us, but the scare was enough to keep us away from his windows thereafter. That was to be our one and only brush with Juan Carlos's strange life.

With the town completely ostracizing the couple and the antique shop having failed due to lack of patronage, Juan Carlos put up his family home for sale within a year. He and his Mexican partner moved away. No one ever heard from him again.

Twenty Two

MISTER LUM AND LOUISE

A few years after Leon's and Pearl's anatomy lessons in the cloakroom and a few months after my father's one-time admonition while quail hunting not to get girls pregnant, my friend Charles and I were learning to drive a car. We were about to turn 15, which was the legal age to get a driver's license in 1946. We took every opportunity we could to practice driving. The best was when Charles's father would let us drive him on his salesman rounds.

Charles's father's nickname was Lum. How he got that name I never knew. Most everybody in Greenville and surrounding Butler County knew Mister Lum. He was a man who lived by his wits. Mister Lum sold or traded just about anything to make his living. The back seat of his two-door 1939 Chevrolet coupe was piled with cloth samples and catalogs for shoes, hats, gloves, overcoats, suits and other clothing items, plus colorful catalogs for an array of seeds, flowers and shrubs. On top of all that, he carried bulk cloth for making clothes. You name it and Mister Lum either had it in the back seat or he could measure you for it on the spot, fill out an order form and have your order in the mail on the same day. All those samples, materials and catalogs formed a huge amorphous mass in that back seat, which either Charles or I would have to sit on while the other one drove.

In addition to selling nearly anything you could order by mail, Mister Lum would trade for anything. Charles never wore the same wristwatch for more than a month before Mister Lum would trade it for something -- anything. One time I watched Mister Lum trade Charles's wristwatch along with an old rowboat he had on a trailer behind the car. He threw in a new Sunday suit, measuring the man for it while standing in a ditch on the edge of a cotton field. In return, Mister Lum got 11 gallons of honey, an old horse and three bushels of sweet potatoes. He had traded houses, cars, boats, horses, pigs, cows, all sorts of vegetables, tools, tractors, wagons and on and on down an endless list of unrelated things, animate and inanimate. Their yard was filled with stuff he had taken in trade and hoped to trade again.

One piece of business I have not mentioned was one of Mister Lum's mainstays. That was burial insurance. He and Mister Hudson were the two burial insurance agents in town. You will meet Mister Hudson at Miss May's boarding house later. Brown Service Burial insurance sold for 10 cents a week. The tough thing about the burial insurance business was that the agent, Mister Lum in this case, had to collect a dime each and every week and give a stamp in exchange for the dime. The owner of the policy then put the stamp in a book, and when it was full he or she would get a certificate of paid-up burial insurance. I never was sure how long it took to pay off a policy, but my father calculated that if you paid out the whole thing it would cost much more than a fine burial would cost in cash. The policy was a good deal financially only if you died prematurely. All that aside, burial insurance at a dime a week was popular among whites and blacks, and Mister Lum was big in that business. I'm sure he saw it as a wonderful lead-in for all of the other things he sold and traded.

Mister Lum And Louise

Charles and I loved it because Mister Lum let us rotate driving his car on rounds while he kept books in the front seat. He would jump in and out as we moved house to house down the backstreets of Greenville. Then we would drive into the country where the houses spaced out between longer stretches of road, which we preferred for driving practice. On these rides, Mister Lum carried on a constant conversation on almost any topic, most of which centered on the price and value of nearly everything. He was encyclopedic on the values and prices and would recount the great trades and deals of his life as we drove from house to house.

One day, with no advance notice, we pulled up to the house where Louise and Pearl lived. Charles and I looked at each other and smirked. There we were, actually parked on the side of the road in front of the house of Greenville's best known whore and her daughter. We were wide eyed and trying our best not to burst out laughing.

Mister Lum said nothing, but got out of the car and jumped across the clay ditch that ran along the side of the road. He had to take one of those long awkward jump-steps to clear it and at the same time get over the high Johnson grass that filled the ditch. With a good jump over the grass, he landed at the edge of Louise's clean-swept front yard.

The frame house had never been painted. It was built on a raised foundation, so looking underneath it we could see all the way through to the backyard. Chickens and a couple of hound dogs lived up under there. The high front porch had a swing at one end and two front doors.

On his way to the front steps, Mister Lum stepped in some chicken dung. He stopped to clean the sole of his shoe with a stick. He stood on the ground and leaned against the high front porch scraping and scraping for the longest time, making a lot more out of it than seemed necessary. The old hound wobbled up and sniffed out the situation carefully, then ambled on back up under the house unimpressed.

Charles and I couldn't figure out what was going on, but it later occurred to me that stepping in chicken mess gave Mister Lum the perfect excuse not to go up on Louise's porch. No matter who lived there, you didn't track poop up on the porch. By keeping a respectable distance from this house of ill repute, Mister Lum was saying to Charles and me, "Look, this is very professional. I am here on burial insurance business, nothing more. I am standing in the front yard, not even on the steps and *certainly* not on the porch itself and *most certainly* not near Louise's front door and *obviously* not in her living room or *anywhere near* those things that go on here." If Mister Lum had been talking I am sure that's what he was trying to tell us by not going up on the porch.

Mister Lum finally knocked on the floorboards of the front porch. In a few minutes, Louise appeared at the door in a thin negligee open down the front. She smiled broadly at Mister Lum and said in a no-fooling kind of voice, "Lum, honey, what on earth you doing standing down there on the ground? Honey, come up on the porch."

Mister Lum's face turned crimson. Pointing toward the car, he said, in a halting voice, "Got my son, uh, his friend with me, uh, stepped in this chicken mess... here to collect on the policy." Louise leaned down to see us in the car and when she did, the negligee fell away from her body and both her breasts appeared. In toto. Full on nudity. I was riveted. Then she waved at us all friendly, and I tried to grin like nothing was wrong. I'm sure I looked like the Cheshire cat with that forced smile on my face. I could hardly breathe. I felt my heart beat in my neck. My face flushed.

Louise disappeared into the house. In a minute she returned and leaned down even lower to give Mister Lum a dime. Again,

Mister Lum And Louise

we got an eyeful. It was the first time I ever saw female breasts, the same for Charles. Daughter Pearl had given us our first look at the lower parts of the female anatomy, and now Momma had introduced us to the upper.

Meanwhile, it was business as usual for Mister Lum.

"Ain't you going to pay for Pearl's policy?" he asked Louise.

"Hell no, she's gonna pay her own burial policy from now on," she answered. "Pearl's big enough to shake her own ass now."

Pearl came to the other front door and peered out onto the porch. "Hey, Mister Lum," she said. "Momma told me I was gonna pay my own burial insurance from now on. Just a minute. I'll get a dime."

She reappeared and handed Mister Lum a dime, then looked toward the car, "Hey, boys," she called in our direction. "Come see me when you can. I'll show you some fun."

"Hey, Pearl," was all we could manage. Charles and I looked at each other. I don't know what color my face was but Charles's was deep red.

Despite Pearl's open invitation for sex, we declined. The idea of paid-sex combined with the fears of VD made sure of that, not to mention the Baptists' promise of going to hell for an eternity for lying down with a whore. God only knew what punishment having paid-sex with the teenage daughter of a whore would be. We weren't going there.

We never saw Pearl again. She had dropped out of school the year we delivered Mister Lum to the house to collect burial insurance premiums. I always wondered what happened to her.

Twenty Three

Miss Irene and Mister Hudson

After my mother died, my father arranged for me to eat supper at Miss May's boarding house whenever he was on the road for his job as agricultural agent with the L&N Railroad. Some weeks, he had to be out of town several nights; other weeks he traveled locally and was home at night. I went everywhere in town on my bicycle, so late in the afternoon after basketball practice when Daddy was out of town, I pedaled over to Miss May's and sat on the porch with all the boarders waiting for the supper bell to ring.

I enjoyed the late afternoons as the sun went down across the front railing of the porch. As the sun set, the crickets and kaydydids started their high-pitched hum with intermittent and curious crescendos and decrescendos. The changing tones and volume sounded like a musical conductor was leading them in a chorus. The moments of silence fascinated me especially. Why did the humming stop? What caused it? Why did it start back up? How did the insects all know at the same time when to start and stop?

Miss May rang the dinner bell, so the group moved from the porch to the large table in the dining room. I listened as the adults talked about their day. Most of them lived in the upstairs rooms of the boarding house. There were two grammar school teachers still looking for apartments and Dr. Demming the new dentist who had just moved to town. He was already making eyes at another boarder Miss Dunn, the high school music teacher. Next to Miss Dunn sat Mister Stubby McAdams, the county clerk. Due to a broken hip years earlier, one of Stubby's legs was shorter than the other (hence the name) which made him dip and rise when he walked. The odd gait made him look even shorter than he was already. Miss May's unmarried niece also lived there and helped out with the cooking and serving. Miss May's husband had died a few years before of chronic lung disease.

There was Miss Irene, an old maid, who worked at city hall and kept track of the water bills for the city. She was at least in her mid 60s and had never married. According to my father, who filled me in on all the regulars at Miss May's, Miss Irene had never had a "beau" or "suitor," as they were called. Miss Irene lived in a room a few blocks away and walked over for the evening meal and then walked alone back to her room. I never heard her join in any conversation. If anyone tried to engage her, she would nod pleasantly and smile and then look away.

Then there was Mister Hudson who drove a Hudson car. That baffled me: a Hudson driving a Hudson. Mister Hudson talked a lot and held the center of attention. He sold life and burial insurance and was Mister Lum's biggest competitor. Burial insurance was a big thing in those times. Mister Hudson, like Mister Lum, went house to house weekly to collect a dime and give the policyholder a stamp to be pasted in their burial insurance booklet. I suppose the policy could be paid in full, but most people didn't. Most people wouldn't want to be even a dime ahead if they died suddenly. That was Mister Hudson's theory on why they preferred the weekly installments.

Miss Irene And Mister Hudson

At the supper table, Mister Hudson always sat between Dr. Dimming and Miss Irene. I never heard Mister Hudson and Miss Irene speak to each other, although Mister Hudson would pull out the chair for her to be seated. That was not unusual, since most gentlemen did that for ladies.

The food was always delicious. A typical supper would include fried chicken, green beans, turnip greens, black-eyed peas, fried corn, mashed potatoes, potato salad, cornbread or biscuits and a dessert, usually banana pudding. We passed the large bowls around the table for everyone to serve themselves. There was always a meat, several vegetables and a dessert, all for 35 cents. Occasionally, we had a full breakfast for supper – eggs, grits, bacon, biscuits and jams, the whole works. That was my favorite.

Later that year as my classmates began to pass their 15th birthdays, friends began getting their driver's licenses. I was the youngest in my age group, so I had to ride in their cars when we went out. Our favorite jaunt was to see a picture show at the Ritz Theater, ride around town a bit and then head to Tom's Drive-in and Bus Station at the top of the hill. The movie cost a dime. A hamburger at Tom's also cost a dime and a Coke was a nickel.

These were our earliest romantic efforts with girls. There was not yet any pairing of boy with girl; outings were still group affairs. But we liked to make the group large so we could jam as many as possible into the car. That meant the girls had to sit close or even on our laps and intoxicate us with perfume, incredibly soft bodies and desire. While the female proximity was bliss, these were still confusing occasions. Fears of syphilis and pregnancy and hellfire and damnation always lurked just beneath our consciousness, warring with our ever-increasing natural feelings and urges. However, beyond those fears there was one more overriding, never-stated-but-clearly-understood, absolute guiding rule regarding teenage sex: Nice girls don't put out. Ever. Putting out was against the law for nice girls, and nice boys knew that. But we never gave up trying.

I remember one particular night vividly. There were seven of us in John's Oldsmobile, three boys and four girls. We had skipped the movie, cruised around town a bit and then headed right up to Tom's Drive-in. We pulled into one of the six parking places reserved for drive-in food in front of the concrete block diner/bus station. The waitress was Sally Mayhew from the grade ahead of us in high school. Since none of us had much money, we split hamburgers with the girls and ordered Cokes all around for a nickel each.

Just as we ordered our food, Mister Hudson pulled up in the parking place next to ours, honked his horn for service and slid down deep in his seat until the top of his head was barely visible. He didn't look our way. I was sitting at the window in the back seat and had a clear view of his car only a few feet away.

In a few minutes, Frog came hobbling out to our car with our tray of food. It was obvious Frog was in over his head. Tom, the owner, Frog's 1933 classmate, was trying to help him out. Frog couldn't take orders, but he was being trained to deliver food. He forgot one of our hamburgers and two of the Cokes, so it took him several trips. He kept mumbling to himself as he went back and forth.

Just after Frog brought our last Coke out to the car, I turned toward Mister Hudson's car. There, rising up from the floorboard of the rear seat for a moment so fleeting that I nearly missed seeing her, was the top of Miss Irene's head. She reached over the front seat and took a bottle of Coke from Mister Hudson. As she was about to slide back to the floorboard, her eyes caught mine. The look she gave me was not so much horror as "Oh, my God.

Miss Irene And Mister Hudson

You have seen me. You, you young boy, who will tell everyone." It was not fear, but sadness, I saw. In that instant, I wanted to tell her that her secret was safe. I wanted her to know that if, for whatever strange and incomprehensible reason, she had to hide her feelings for Mister Hudson, I wouldn't breathe it to a soul. And I haven't until now, nearly 70 years later.

We looked at each other for only a moment, then she disappeared back down onto the floorboard of the back seat. Mister Hudson immediately cranked up the car, backed out and headed down the road away from town. I guessed Miss Irene told him I had seen her. Just as they pulled out onto the highway, a Trailways bus pulled in. The noise and fumes and hiss of the air brakes distracted my thoughts momentarily, but the strange encounter would continue to baffle me for years to come.

After that night at Tom's Drive-in, Miss Irene didn't come to supper at Miss May's for over a week. Mister Hudson was there in his regular seat, however, and continued to hold court as the center of attention each night.

When Miss Irene finally did reappear, she sat quietly in her same seat next to Mister Hudson and said nothing. On one occasion, she looked at me and smiled faintly. I never talked to her and she never talked to me.

A few years later when I was back home from college on Christmas vacation, someone told me Miss Irene had died. A few years after that, Mister Hudson dropped dead from a heart attack. Neither had ever married. What deep, dark secret kept Miss Irene and Mister Hudson in the shadows? I'll never know. Whatever it was, I suppose both died with their secret intact. Even in small towns, sometimes mysteries are forever buried.

Twenty Four

WILDCATS AND COUNTRY BOYS

L eon, as you now know, was a country boy. A boy was "country" if he rode a school bus to and from school. Both schools I attended -- the W.O. Parmer Grammar School and Greenville High School -- were county schools. Over half the students came from farms in the surrounding county, so twice each day more than a dozen yellow buses filled with hundreds of students pulled in or out of the large parking lot in front of the football stadium.

The great majority of country boys and girls came from uneducated parents and lived in abject poverty. The classic book *Let Us Now Praise Famous Men*, written by James Agee with photographs by Walker Evans, depicts the lives of such poor tenant farmers. Those powerful photographs, taken only one county away, could have been some of my classmates.

Just as we called the boys from outside of town "country," they called any boy from town a "city boy." The relationships weren't always contentious, however. All of us town boys knew a few country boys we called friends. We visited in their homes, as they did in ours.

Clifton K. Meador M.D.

A few of the country boys had second-hand pickup trucks of their own. Leon, who had taught us anatomy lessons with Pearl in the cloakroom in sixth grade, now had his own pickup truck, a beat-up 1933 Ford. Most of the paint was peeling off, the roof was rusting around the edges, and there were dents all over the body. Even so, we envied Leon that pickup, just as we did the now-well-worn Army shirt he still wore proudly every day.

One Saturday, Leon and two of his buddies drove into town. They pulled a large metal cage out of the back of the truck onto the courthouse lawn. Inside was a captured, furious bobcat. Leon had set some traps and caught the cat somewhere deep in the swamps north of town. He was proud that it was male. He said tomcats were more vicious than females and much harder to trap. In Leon's mind, he had caught a prize.

The slightest movement toward the cage sent the cat into a frenzy of clawing and hissing. Leon encouraged all this drama by poking a stick at it, making sure the cat stayed riled up. I shuddered to think what the attack might be like if the wildcat got loose.

The cat drew crowd after crowd in front of the courthouse that Saturday afternoon, until Leon and his buddies hauled it away in his truck. The following week, we learned what the threesome had done with it. At recess on Monday, Leon gathered a crowd around him and, as usual, began rolling a Bull Durham cigarette using just one hand and his teeth. Leon had a knack for rolling cigarettes and for storytelling. He might have made it on the stage in another time and place.

First, Leon said, they got a big hemp sack and pulled it over the opening of the cage. By working on all sides, he and his buddies managed to force that wildcat into the sack and tie the opening. You can bet it was a fight, he told us, showing off the red scratches on both arms where the cat clawed him. Once inside the sack, the cat went even more berserk. It took about an hour before it finally gave up and settled down. Once it did, they stuffed the sack with the cat inside into a large suitcase and closed the lid.

Then Leon and his buddies drove the suitcase out onto a long country road with side roads intersecting it ever so often. On one of the side roads, but in full view of the main road, they placed it in front of a rural mailbox. Leon then backed his truck up the side road where he had a clear view of the main road and the suitcase, but no one could see him. They waited for the first car to come along the main road.

Leon told us, "I knowed exactly what was going to happen."

In a few minutes, a 1940 four-door Buick packed with country people heading into town came down the road. At first, the car ran past the suitcase but then stopped and backed up. As Leon predicted, a man jumped out, grabbed the suitcase and squeezed back into the crowded car. At this point in telling his story, Leon was already laughing so hard he could barely talk.

After the man picked up the suitcase, Leon pulled his truck onto the main road and followed at a safe distance behind the Buick. Soon the Buick started to weave from one side of the road to another. In a few moments, one man jumped out of the back door on the right and then another jumped out on the left. The car ran off and on the road and in and out of ditches and eventually raced out into a cotton field where it abruptly stopped. Every door came flying open, spilling the remaining three passengers and the driver who all ran screaming from the abandoned car. The cat completed the exodus, raced across the field and disappeared into the woods.

By this time, our recess group was hysterical with laughter. We asked Leon to tell it again, as he did happily that day and on many more to come. The more he told it, the harder he laughed.

Clifton K. Meador M.D.

Country boys lived closer to the real and raw world than us town boys. They knew hog-killing time in the winter, ringing chicken necks for dinner, castrating young bulls to make steers and butchering cows and sheep for meat. They knew and shared all the vivid details of breeding horses, cows and pigs. Hunting, shooting and killing something were part of every week. Even their pranks had a gritty side. So putting a wildcat in a croaker sack and stuffing him in a suitcase, although imaginative, was not that special for country boys. I've since heard of others pulling the same prank, so I'm not sure if Leon originated this or heard about it and decided to copy. In either case, he loved the uproar it caused, not to mention telling the story over and over.

"You know," Leon would always say, "I just don't know anybody who could resist pickin' up a suitcase sitting on the side of a country road."

Twenty Five

GRADY AND LUCY

Grady Mitchell was one of Leon's buddies. Actually, he was more than a buddy; he was Leon's sidekick. Among other characteristics, Grady wore a large key ring attached to his belt. Grady said he could unlock any lock and delighted in showing you he could. The key ring gave him an air of authority.

Grady was best known for the many expressions he made up and used frequently. Usually these expressions made little or no sense, but they always got a laugh. His most enigmatic, which he applied when talking about someone he didn't like, went, "If I had a dog that looked like him, I'd shave his ass and make him walk backwards." Now go figure that one. He had many others. If someone doubted something he said, he would say, "If that ain't so, I'll kiss your ass in front of the Ritz Theater and give you five minutes to draw a crowd."

Grady was always Leon's partner in crime or pranks and loved to recount those tales afterwards. Leon delighted in pulling pranks, especially on us city boys. Grady told the story over and over at recess about his night with Leon, Warren and Philip. Warren and Philip were city boys.

Clifton K. Meador M.D.

"Leon approached Warren and Philip," Grady began. "He told them about this girl Lucy and how he had spent the night with her. How she was a real beauty. Lived on a farm near Fort Deposit. Leon told them how she took him and his two buddies on for a night of wild fun. How Lucy's father worked at the mill so he was gone every night. Just left Lucy at home alone."

Grady went on with the story. "Leon persuaded Warren and Philip to go with him to see Lucy one night. He invited me to come along, too. Leon guaranteed every one of us would get our turn. Got Warren to drive his father's car.

"We drove up toward Lucy's. Way out in the country. The house was pitch dark. Leon told Warren he should park down the road a bit just in case. Then the four of us walked up the hill to the house.

"Just as we were about to go up the front steps, the door flew open. A big man with a shotgun charged out onto the porch. 'What the hell?!' the man shouted, 'You come after my daughter?!? I'm gon' shoot yo' asses!' The man fired two quick shots -- *boom, boom!* Kept yellin' at us while reloadin' to shoot again.

"Leon, Warren and Philip took off across a cornfield, running' hard as they could. You could hear cornstalks poppin' and crunching' all the way across that field. They ran for nearly half mile before they stopped.

"Then another man yelled, 'There they go! Shoot 'em! Shoot 'em!' Then two more shots -- *boom, boom!* I heard Leon yell out that he saw me get hit. Saw me fall to the ground.

"Well, Warren and Philip were all tore up. Scratched and bleeding' from the cornstalks hittin' their arms and faces. They just stood there breathin' hard and askin' 'What we gonna do? What we gonna do?' Leon told them I'd been hit. How they had to get the car and come pick me up.

140

Grady And Lucy

"I was lying' on the ground somewhere between the house and cornfield. I heard Warren speed towards me and slam on the brakes. Leon jumped out the car. Dragged me into the back seat. Off we raced to the hospital.

"When we got to the hospital, Joycey Mayhand and another nurse helped Leon drag me onto a stretcher and pull me into the door. Warren and Philip tried to follow, but Joyce told them to sit in the waitin' room.

"In a few minutes, Joyce came back into the waitin' room. She said, 'Boys, hate to tell you but Grady's dead.'"

Leon usually took over the storytelling from here. "Warren jumped right up out of his seat," Leon said. "He knelt down and started prayin'. Kept sayin' he had to leave town. Maybe go to California or somewhere. Philip then knelt down and started prayin' out loud."

Leon, laughing and talking at the same time, said, "You see, there wasn't no man. Grady never got shot. Joyce and the other nurse agreed ahead of time to play along. We had half the football team hidin' in the house to watch the whole made-up thing. One of them dressed up like an old man. Worse part is there wasn't even any Lucy."

We all laughed so hard. I thought my sides would split. "We wondered how Warren and Philip got all those scratches on their arms and faces," somebody in the group said. "They made up something about rabbit hunting in some thick brush."

Of course, as funny as the story was, my friends Charles and John and I were all thinking the same thing. Charles turned to us and whispered, "I sure am glad Leon didn't ask *us* to go to Lucy's that night." We all nodded knowingly.

Twenty Six

Rabbit Hunting with Tootsie

Although I worked with both Tootsie and Roosevelt, I came to know Tootsie the best.

Tootsie was tall at 6 feet 4. Being part Indian and part black, he reminded me of the character Punjab in the *Little Orphan Annie* comic strip. He wore a large handlebar moustache that drooped down each corner of his mouth. All he needed was a turban to resemble characters in Rudyard Kipling's stories of India. Tootsie was also a wise man. He was a great judge of character and taught me much about how to live with people. At times, he could even delve into the metaphysical.

While Roosevelt was all about women, Tootsie loved hunting. Rabbit hunting was his favorite, and he took me with him several times. Tootsie's hound dog was named "Old Man." Old Man was 11 years old and looked his age, for a dog. In his youth, Old Man had been a coonhound. The scars around his head and neck came from fights with raccoons and possums. He had survived all the fights, but only succeeded in killing several possums. Coons rarely lose fights with dogs. They escape up a tree after wounding or killing the dog. Old Man was now too old to fight, so Tootsie used him just for rabbit hunting.

I picked up Tootsie at his house in Baptist Hill, the black section of town to the south. He lived at the edge where the town began turning into the countryside. Tootsie's house was set back from the road in the middle of five acres of land. He had fenced in a large section for his pig farm and adjacent cornfield.

As I pulled away from Tootsie's house, he began to tell me stories. "You remember old Fred, who comes by Planters from time to time. He's the head janitor at the courthouse." Tootsie paused to cut a piece of tobacco off a plug he carried in his overalls. Holding the plug with his knife and hand, he slid the piece into his mouth, chewing it around until he got it settled into a pouch between his gum and cheek. This took several moments. After he got the piece nestled in his right jaw, he went on.

"Well, Fred tells me about Miss Ethyl up at the courthouse. How she caught Judge Scranton and his new secretary up on his desk. Right there 'fo God and everybody. Doin' his business." Tootsie laughed and shook his head.

"Fred said Miss Ethyl had her own eyes set on the judge. So she got real mad. Went around tellin' everybody 'bout what she found." Tootsie got me laughing with him.

"There ain't no anger worse than a mad woman. Specially if she's let down by a man. Miss Ethyl stay mad. She tell everybody who come in the courthouse." Tootsie, still grinning, shook his head in disbelief. "Po' Judge. He's ruint."

Tootsie spit some tobacco juice out the window and continued. "There ain't no explanation for what the judge did. Fred say if you bait a man trap with poontang you gonna catch all sorts – lawyers,

Rabbit Hunting With Tootsie

doctors, store owners, even probate judges. The way Roosevelt carries on with women, it's a wonder he ain't been shot by some woman."

Tootsie knew everyone in town and a story about most of them. He did not care much for preachers. Roosevelt's preacher had run off with the collection money one Sunday and he told Tootsie the story. "Some people do stupid things," Tootsie said. "Roosevelt said they wanted to borrow a car to go get the preacher and bring him back home. He had run off with the collection and one of the women in the church. Probably in the next county by the time they figured it out. They asked Mister William at the Sinclair station to borrow his pickup so they could go get the preacher. Mister William say 'no.' He say the money would be gone and ain't no use goin' to get the preacher except to get in trouble. He asked why they want to get the preacher back.

"You ain't gonna believe what Roosevelt said." Tootsie paused, throwing the chewing tobacco wad out the car window and cutting a new bite. "Roosevelt said they gonna catch the preacher and bring him back to the church. Roosevelt said they gonna make him *preach it out, preach out the money they stole!*" By this time Tootsie is laughing so hard, he can barely talk. "I tell you, between stealin' money and runnin' off with women, some preachers are a sorry lot."

When we got to the field for our hunt, Tootsie untied Old Man from his rope leash and turned him loose. Soon that coondog was running in circles in the deep brush and grass. We were following close behind, when all of a sudden a white rabbit darted across an open space. Tootsie stopped and made a loud whistle with his fingers in his mouth. The rabbit stopped completely still, looking right and left. That's when Tootsie took his shot. Old Man raced to the dead rabbit, brought it up to Tootsie and dropped it at his feet.

"Good boy, Old Man, good boy," Tootsie said patting the dog on the head.

I was puzzled by Tootsie's whistling at the rabbit before he shot. "You see," Tootsie explained, "before a rabbit runs, he has to stop and roll up his britches leg. When he hears me whistle, he knows it's time to roll up his britches. So he stops. That's when I shoot him. Happens every time. Try it."

At first I didn't believe him, but I saw him do it with several more rabbits that day and on later hunts. I never could get it to work for me.

When my mother died in 1945, my 14th year, Tootsie and Roosevelt came up to me at the cemetery and told me how sorry they were. Both men seemed to pay more attention to me on the Saturdays that followed. I stayed close to Tootsie for many years and always dropped by to see him when I came home from college.

On one such visit home several years after I had finished college, Roosevelt told me Tootsie had died. My grief didn't last long. At his age, death was expected. An old friend once told me that grief is like a pan of water set out in the bright sunshine. Like the water, it slowly evaporates leaving the good memories. The good memories of Tootsie still linger.

Twenty Seven

ROOSEVELT TELLS ALL

Despite our fears of pregnancy and syphilis and the prospects of hellfire and damnation, our curiosities and libido continued to gain force. That's where Roosevelt comes in.

As I explained earlier, Roosevelt worked in the back room at Planter's Mercantile where I helped out on Saturdays. Tootsie was in charge, and Roosevelt and I were his assistants. Tootsie was a hard worker and a patient teacher who could talk about life with wisdom well beyond his education. Roosevelt, on the other hand, was none of these things. He was into one subject and one subject only: women.

On Saturdays, Greenville's downtown turned into a swarm of people, 90 percent of them black. The county population was around 90 percent black. Since Saturday was a day off work, the farm laborers and sharecroppers always came to town to shop and socialize. The sidewalks teemed with men, women, and children of all ages, overflowing into the street. Traffic, then still mostly wagons pulled by mules, slowed to a crawl. Despite the throng, there was a strange quietness and courtesy among the crowds, almost a hush.

Clifton K. Meador M.D.

Blacks came like waves into Planter's, and Tootsie and Roosevelt and I waited on them. While the front of the store sold dry goods, the back end where we worked sold staples and items needed on a farm. Whenever a customer would come in, we would fill the order and then call for the senior Mister Haygood who owned the place. As mentioned earlier, Mister Haygood never smiled. He would bring the small black notebook he kept in his hip pocket to record every transaction, as everything was traded on credit against the coming cotton crop. We told him the total for the merchandise, then he talked a bit to the farmer, took out his little notebook and wrote down the farmer's name and the amount of his purchase. The farmer, especially if he were black, would go overboard to be nice to Mister Haygood, thanking him profusely for the loan and promising a good crop and to return to settle when the cotton came in. Mister Haygood knew precisely the acreage of cotton each farmer worked. He also made careful distinction between sharecroppers and tenant farmers, requiring the landowners to assume the debt for the sharecroppers who owned nothing and worked literally for a share of the crop.

Amid all of this throng of people, Roosevelt quietly worked his way through the day with what appeared to be a continuous harem of women. He liked all kinds, young and old, fat and skinny, tall and short, light skinned and dark skinned, talkative and quiet, and even the ugly ones. He loved on them all, and they loved on him back. He was sweet to this one and then another one, all day long managing to somehow avoid dealing with two women at once or getting caught by another. He called them all "Honey" or "Sweetie" or "Sugar" or "Baby" or "Sweet Thing." And the women, dressed in their come-to-town Sunday-best dresses, giggled and nudged up against him, sometimes feigning a slap or a push. Tootsie, who would be trying to wait on a store full of customers, would mumble at him every once in a while, "Get on over here, Roosevelt, and leave them women alone!"

Roosevelt Tells All

My friend John would drop by sometimes on Saturday so we could visit. If we were busy, he would help out for no pay so Tootsie wouldn't fuss at us for talking. As long as I was working, Tootsie didn't care who I talked to. John was purportedly there to see me, but he was really there to see Roosevelt. He was convinced that Roosevelt was the leading authority on women and sex, and I agreed. John thought we could learn a lot from Roosevelt. He got the bright idea to ask Roosevelt what it felt like. He wasn't subtle about it.

"Roosevelt, what does it feel like?" John just came right out one day and asked him.

Roosevelt, looking a little surprised, answered, "What you mean? Get on 'way from me."

John kept at him. "Aw, come on Roosevelt," he kept saying. But each time it was the same answer: "Get on 'way from me," Roosevelt said. "You ain't gonna get me in any trouble with yo Daddy. Go on outta here."

John tried another tactic. Under his breath -- but loud enough so we could all hear him -- he mumbled that maybe Roosevelt *didn't know* what it felt like. That got a big laugh out of Tootsie.

"He knows," Tootsie said, "but looks like he ain't gonna tell you." Then Tootsie started egging Roosevelt on: "Go on tell 'em. I want to hear it myself."

The banter went on between John and Roosevelt for several visits. Tootsie and I continued to put in our two cents, too. We got more and more insistent. Finally, Roosevelt had had enough. "Alright!" he blurted out. "You keep after me, I'm gonna tell you... I'm gonna tell you exactly."

Clifton K. Meador M.D.

It had been a particularly busy day, but now it was late and the crowds had dwindled. Roosevelt sat down on the curb out by the back of the store. John and I eagerly took our places on either side of him. Tootsie stood behind us, looking right and left, keeping guard. Roosevelt fiddled with some keys as he talked.

"You ever been quail huntin'?" he began. We both nodded yes. "Well, you know how when the dog gets on a point, like he straight as a stovepipe and quiverin' and his tail is all pointed out and his eyes is glazed over, almost like he turned into stone sep you see him breathin' so you knows he alive? And you knows the birds is close by but you don't know where and you begins to move up on the covey and every step you knows might be the one that fires 'em to fly off and you knows that when you do finally break that stick that sets 'em off that you don't know for a minute 'xactly what's goin' on 'cause one bird flies back right at you and two or three flies off to your left and a few flies straight away from you and there's feathers goin' up in the air and in the middle of all that is this loud *whrrrrrrooooommmmmm* sound of the whole covey noise and the dogs is runnin' 'round and jumpin' up in the air......You knows what I'm talkin' 'bout?"

Both of us had witnessed that scene dozens of times. I caught John out of the corner of my eye. He looked like a guppy too long out of water. His mouth gaped open, and he sat motionless, frozen, enthralled. "You been right there, ain't you?" Roosevelt asked, looking at me, then John. "You knows what I'm talkin' 'bout.

"Well, now, just imagine that all that fuss and all that noise and feathers flyin' and guns shootin' and birds flappin' and dogs carryin' on and everything ... imagine ALL that happening' at once ... *then imagine all that comin' out yo' ass!*"

John and I look at each other, mouths wide open. We were dumbfounded, totally absorbed in Roosevelt's vivid, and we hoped

Roosevelt Tells All

accurate, description. Then we heard Tootsie chuckling, and Roosevelt began to laugh. Soon they were doubled over. I looked at John and we exploded in laughter, too. The four of us, infected by each other's laughter, cackled until we could barely breathe.

Between fits of laughing, Tootsie managed to say, "That's pretty good Roosevelt...pretty good."

Twenty Eight

THE 1947 GREENVILLE HIGH SCHOOL

BASKETBALL TEAM

It was mid season and the Greenville High School basketball team had an even record, five wins/five losses. There was a possibility our team would surpass the record of the famous 1933 team that won the Southeast Alabama State Tournament. That was the year Frog was the assistant team manager.

Several Army veterans had returned from the war in '47 aiming to get their high school diplomas. Before they were drafted, these boys had all failed one or two grades in school, so they were much older than us. I had just turned 15 when the season started. Two of the veterans, Kelly Scott and Wert Simmons, were 20. Both were excellent basketball players. I played center and my best friend John played left forward. Leon, now back in school from his bogus stint in the Army, was a substitute guard.

We played all the surrounding small towns in South Alabama – Georgiana, Luvern, Ozark, Enterprise, Pineapple, Camden, Troy and others. On one road trip, we played most of the small towns around Birmingham, losing more than we won.

Clifton K. Meador M.D.

One of the tricks to winning games in small town high schools was getting to know the foibles of the various basketball courts. Each one was different. Most of the courts were located in auditoriums that doubled as gyms, so one goal always hung down in front of a stage. Whenever we came in for a layup, we had to quickly pull up our feet and land like a big bird on the stage behind the goal. This took some practice since the height of the stages varied from one town to the next. In one of the makeshift auditoriums, the court ran east to west and the goals were fastened onto brick walls. As we advanced toward the basket, we had to shoot with one hand and hold the other one straight out to keep from slamming face first into bricks. The only place where we didn't have to play in a converted auditorium was Pineapple High School. The school was so small it didn't have an auditorium. The basketball court was outside. The court was packed clay with goals on posts at each end. We could only play Pineapple in the daytime.

Our team made many great memories that year, but the game against Highland Home wasn't one of them. It was, at once, the most memorable and most forgettable. Highland Home was about 40 miles from Greenville in one of the poorest farming areas. The community was among the hardest hit in the state by the Great Depression, and even in 1947 they had barely begun to recover.

We dressed in our basketball uniforms before we left town and put on our regular clothes over the uniforms. This was common practice since most of the small schools like Highland Home were county schools that had no dressing rooms or showers. Sometimes we took our uniforms with us and changed in an empty classroom.

That night at Highland Home, we slipped out of our street clothes in a classroom and went to warm up. Their team was already on the court, dressed in pitiful uniforms indicative of the hard times. Each player wore an ordinary white undershirt with his

154

The 1947 Greenville High School Basketball Team

number hand-drawn in indelible black ink on the front and back. Some of the undershirts were way too big so that half the numbers were tucked down into their shorts. I guessed the average age of the players to be well into their 20s. We learned later they were all returning veterans.

We raced confidently onto our end the court to warm up. The home team was practicing layups at their end. We soon learned that it didn't really matter which team was on which end, because the converted gym was so small that the center line dividing the court was also the foul line. We're talking an *extremely* short court. As we rebounded off the backboard at one end during the game, we were immediately in the forward court of the other end. Highland Home players were used to this. We weren't.

Adding to our woes was the uneven floor. We had noticed in warmups how the Highland Home players zigzagged as they headed toward a goal. They obviously knew how to dribble effectively across the quirky surface. We didn't. As we dribbled in for a layup, the ball careened off the slanted floor in every direction.

There was one final disadvantage at Highland Home. The ceiling of the auditorium/gym was very low, making outside shots at the goal difficult at best. One of our secret weapons was the long, high-arcing shot, but here we had to toss the ball almost flat. Otherwise, it ricocheted off the ceiling and went out of bounds.

It's no surprise the final score was 76 to 13 in their favor. Most of our points came from foul shots.

After the game, we went back to the classroom to change out of our uniforms. Along the windows were several potted plants. Kelly said he was going to pee in them to retaliate for our humiliating defeat. We talked him out of it.

Clifton K. Meador M.D.

We made it through the season with a 50 percent win record and headed to the Southeast Alabama State Tournament in Andalusia, 50 miles south of Greenville. The winner of that tourney would move on to the state finals in Tuscaloosa. Only the 1933 Greenville team had ever advanced to the state finals.

Coach Eddins and one of the fathers always drove to the games. Two cars carried the whole lot of us, plus equipment and Frog who still came along to out-of-town games. As we loaded up for the trip south to Andalusia, the excitement was palpable. It was one of the larger towns in South Alabama; they had a real gym, not a converted auditorium; and we were trying to repeat history. Frog wore his black and gold jacket with his "G" letter on the front and, as always, his whistle around his neck. He kept saying, "Jess like then. Big ga... Big ga..."

When we arrived, it was obvious we were way out of our league. Most of the teams were almost 100 percent veterans. They were much older, bigger and more skilled than we were. We lost our first game by a margin so large, I've erased it from memory. Highland Home went on to win the sectional tournament and advance to the finals in Tuscaloosa, losing to Montgomery's Sidney Lanier High School.

In the end, our dream of shattering the 1933 Greenville High School basketball team's record remained just that -- a dream. But we had a lot of fun.

Twenty Nine

Mrs. Nathan Henry

Nathan Henry was by far the richest man in Greenville's black community. Some said he was one of the richest men in town.

He and the three undertakers he employed had a steady and profitable burial business, thanks in no small part to the insurance sold by my friend Charles's father Mister Lum and Mister Hudson. Burial insurance provided a reliable source of income to both the black and white funeral homes.

I never met Nathan Henry, but I did meet his second wife, Geraldine.

His first wife died of cancer. Geraldine, a much younger woman, lived with him in a big house just around the corner from the Henry Funeral Home. It was in a black section of town called Baptist Hill. He had begun to pour a lot of money into redecorating the house for his new wife, which is how I came into the picture.

In the summer of 1947, after my junor year in high school and just before my 16th birthday, I worked for Riley Construction Company. In addition to building things, Riley sold all sorts of supplies and tools for home repairs. Most of the time, I drove a pickup truck hauling sand and gravel and other building materials to the construction sites, but I also handled all the orders for venetian blinds. I would go to the home or business, measure the windows or doors, come back to the store and order the blinds. When the blinds arrived, I went back to the home or business and hung them.

One day Geraldine Henry called and wanted to order venetian blinds.

The dirt roads in Baptist Hill were a deep, muddy clay and very slippery even on dry days. Driving to the Henrys', I had to be careful not to slide off into a ditch. This was one of the few times I ever drove into Baptist Hill, although I had been there many times with Daddy to pick up our clean laundry from our maid Mamie's sister.

The white clapboard one-story Henry house sat back from the road. In front of it was a brand new concrete sidewalk, running from one edge of the yard to the other. And there it stopped. There were no other sidewalks in all of Baptist Hill, just dirt ditches in front of all the other houses. Nathan Henry had obviously built his own to spruce up the property. It was a strange sight to see only one sidewalk.

A nice brick walk lead from the sidewalk to the front steps of the house. The Henrys had installed elaborate cream-colored metal awnings above each front window, making the house all the more distinctive in a neighborhood of gray, weatherworn shacks. Here was a substantial structure with shiny new awnings, a brick walk and its very own sidewalk surrounded on all sides by ramshackle cottages.

Geraldine Henry met me at the door. She was dressed like she was going to a party or to church. She wore a string of pearls around her neck, a pretty white blouse and a soft blue cashmere sweater tied around her shoulders. I noticed she wore high heels and silk stockings. She looked like no other black woman I had ever seen. I stepped back to take her all in.

"Please come right in. You must be from Riley Construction," she said, enunciating every word crisply and clearly. Her accent sounded polished like I imagined someone from the North might talk. She sounded like no other black woman I had ever heard.

She began to show me one window after another, telling me the colors she wanted for the blinds. She had French doors at the back of the house, opening onto a brick patio with chairs and a metal table. The backyard was filled with flowering bushes and planted pots and surrounded with a painted white privacy fence.

After I measured the windows and recorded the measurements, she held me back a few moments to tell me about herself. She had graduated from Tuskegee Institute (now Tuskegee University) with a major in history and a minor in English. She had just begun to teach at the new all-black junior college south of town.

I sat in awe. Here was a black woman like no other. Well spoken. A college graduate. A college teacher. Her house and yard beautifully decorated. It could have been any house in the nicest white section of town. But here it sat in the middle of poverty, surrounded by dilapidated shanties in every direction. And to cap it all off, that single strip of concrete sidewalk that stopped at the side edges of the front yard. I was dumbstruck.

A few weeks later when I returned to hang the venetian blinds, she again met me at the front door. After I finished the job, she offered me a cup of coffee. I thought it only polite to accept. We sat for several minutes in her living room telling each other tidbits about our lives. She seemed lonely for conversation. I felt awkward and ill at ease. Slowly I began to relax as I answered her questions about myself and my family. I found myself addressing her as "Mrs. Henry." For a few brief moments and for the first time in my life, I had closed the unbridgeable gulf that existed between white and black.

I would like to say those moments changed something in me forever. Maybe they did. But this was Greenville, Alabama, in 1947. In the time it took to say goodbye, walk down the brick walk and cross over that one patch of concrete sidewalk to my pickup truck, I was back in the real world of separation and segregation. I never saw Mrs. Nathan Henry again, but I never forgot her either.

Thirty

THE FINAL CURTAIN: THE BLUE AND GREY PARADE

We were approaching the end of high school. A few of us had begun to talk about college. I had just turned 16, having skipped a grade, and was more and more ready to move on into the next phases of my life. I began to reflect on my years in Greenville and the people I knew and loved. I had a feeling I would soon be leaving the town and many of them behind.

When the governor of the State of Alabama invited the band to come to Montgomery to march in the 1947 Blue and Grey parade, I knew it would be a high point, a climax of my time in Greenville. The parade preceded the Blue and Grey Football Classic, an annual college football all-star game held in Alabama around Christmas at the Cramton Bowl. Only seniors played in this game, coming from colleges throughout the South and North. This was only the event's second season.

It was a big deal all around, not to mention a championship game commemorating the war of all wars, the War Between the States. At the time, I thought being a part of it was one of the highest honors that could be paid a citizen of Alabama. In my mind, we were not only to represent our school, Greenville and the state of Alabama, but also the South and the whole defeated Confederate States of America.

To understand what this event meant to me, you have to grasp the setting and imagine what it was like to be that boy of 16 playing second trombone in the Quarter Million Dollar Greenville High School Black and Gold Marching Band. The time was Dec. 26, 1947. World War II had just ended two years before. We had longed to be a part of that war whose romanticized images filled the newsreels and our heads. Being too young or otherwise ineligible to serve was grave disappointment to us teens. Being part of anything we saw as patriotic, even a football parade, thrilled us immensely.

Then there were the girls -- scantily clad girls at that. Going with the band to Montgomery meant majorettes and cheerleaders decked out in those skimpy outfits Reverend Morgan had so eloquently warned us about. The rich combination of sex and patriotism promised by this parade was everything my small-town, 16-year-old self had ever dreamed.

The parade would end at the stadium with a march around the entire track in front of 25,000 screaming fans. It would be the most people in one place I had ever seen, a crowd five times the population of Greenville. Along the route, we would travel the important streets in our state's capital city, past big buildings and landmarks and cheering people. We were heady at the prospect.

On the day of the parade, several dozen high school bands lined up in the backstreets of Montgomery ready to move out onto the route. The majorettes were turning and twirling and showing everything they could, parts that Reverend Morgan, in his tirades about fornication, had made sure we would notice. The cheerleaders were there, too, with their short skirts and well-padded chests. The flag bearers struggled to contain their flags, which were blowing out nearly straight in the cold December breeze. Sounds of instruments being tuned and drums being drummed by all those bands filled the air, the sounds rising and falling in the whipping wind.

Knowing it would be a long afternoon of marching, I had wisely filled my 16-year-old stomach with a fully loaded Chris's hot dog and a Royal Crown Cola, called an "R-O-C." A fully loaded Chris's hot dog in Montgomery was, and always will be, the gold standard for hot dogs. It had mustard of a special sort, thick Heinz ketchup, onions, relish and sauerkraut like I have never had anywhere else in all the years since. The sauerkraut had a distinctive sour taste that made my jaw ache a bit. It was delicious.

Finally, it was time to start. With the taste of that Chris's fully loaded hot dog still in my mouth and the comfort of a full stomach, I started in step with the band as we marched out onto the main parade route. Soon we turned the corner of Capital Square. Then we passed the dark green bronze fountain, where water gushed through the mouths of fish and small boys in great spouts. In later years, I learned that fountain was where Zelda and F. Scott Fitzgerald jumped in drunk and naked in the 1920s. At the time of the parade, however, all I knew was that it looked like pictures I had seen of faraway Rome.

As the band rounded the fountain, we could feel a cold mist from the water blowing around us. Although the winter sun offered little heat on this cloudless day, the mist felt good. You can work up a sweat in a band uniform with all the marching and concentrating and musical effort.

But just as I was reveling in the cool shower and the sight of the beautiful fountain and the crowds and the satisfaction of the fully loaded Chris's hotdog, the majorettes once again stepped center stage into my consciousness. Of course, the majorettes were never far from my consciousness. There they were twirling and turning and bouncing every part that would bounce. It was no wonder that the Reverend Morgan had to force himself to "look away!" from all of that. I can't tell you how happy I was to be playing second trombone and having the great privilege of looking at the behinds and bare legs of six beautiful teenage girls. There, for only the line of trombones to see, were the tantalizing rears of the majorettes and the hourglass shapes formed by their breasts, waists, hips and thighs. Add to all that the blowing hair and the occasional whiffs of perfume drifting ever so faintly backwards. In those moments, which were frequent, everything else vanished. There is something paralytic to teenage boys in perfumes, especially wafting off majorettes.

Beyond the fountain, huge crowds lined the route as it curved into broad Dexter Avenue, the wide street that heads directly up the long, slow hill to the state capital building. As we rounded that curve, all at once we saw it -- that stark white edifice. The capital of the grand State of Alabama which, of course, was also the first capital of the defeated Nation of the Confederates States of America, a defeat still stinging to many in the South. With the view ahead and the crowds lining the streets and the faint sounds of distant drums of all the other bands, my 16-year-old heart pounded in my chest and the hair on my neck stood up.

Then began the long march up Dexter Avenue, moving ever slowly toward that white building that sat on a hill higher than any other in Montgomery. As the view of the capital became more distinct, you could see its columns, one by one. You could see that second column from the left and know for certain it was where Jefferson Davis had stood only 86 years before, right there on that golden star, as he took the oath of office to become the first and only president of the then undefeated Nation of the Confederate States of America. Years earlier, I had stood on that star and looked down Dexter Avenue, knowing I was seeing the same view Davis had once seen. My father had told me that. He had stood there with me and looked out across Montgomery, both of us taking in the same identical view that Jefferson Davis did in 1861.

The Final Curtain: The Blue And Grey Parade

Seeing that gold star again stirred many emotions in me. In the mind of this 16-year-old Southern boy, who in his lifetime had known only one Yankee, who just wished he could have been there, fought in that war, maybe even been wounded like one great grandfather was in the Wilderness. Maybe gone to Virginia with another great grandfather who also fought in the Wilderness. God, what a name for a place to be wounded -- just listen to the pure poetry of it: "wounded in the Wilderness." Maybe he could even have gone to federal prison for captured Confederate soldiers like another of his great grandfathers, the one who had survived dreadful Shiloh with two brothers, only to come home and die of smallpox along with one of his brothers. Memories of the often-told family stories went in and out of my mind. Above all, I yearned for the glory of what going to war might have meant to a boy of 16, not knowing or even considering the other side of the issues of that war and the shame of some of those causes or the God-awfulness and horror and terror of real combat. Those realizations would come much later.

As the Quarter Million Dollar Greenville High School Black and Gold Marching band progressed up Dexter Avenue past the waving and cheering crowds, we could hear dozens of Rebel yells called out. They lifted our hearts and boosted our Southern pride. Moving on up the hill, now noticeably a hill requiring greater and greater effort, we were in front of the Dexter Avenue Baptist Church. Little did we know that we were passing the church that in later years would become the pulpit for a man named Martin Luther King, Jr. and a symbol for the civil rights movement. The capital building was so close that it cast a large morning shadow over the church. As we marched by, none of us had the slightest premonition of things to come. We couldn't imagine that a civil rights monument would someday be placed in back of that church commemorating all those who were killed in the name of equality and human dignity. Those issues were for another day and time, buried for now in the brutal reality of absolute segregation of the races.

Clifton K. Meador M.D.

Beyond the church, the band pulled up to the bottom of the long stairway up the steep hill. All the dignitaries had assembled on the reviewing stand. The Quarter Million Dollar Black and Gold Greenville High School Marching Band was sounding off its drums -- rrrrummp dump, rrrummp dump, rrrrrrrr rump-dump. This was our lead-in to *Dixie*, which every band that day must have played. With *Dixie* blaring from my trombone, and that gold star now up the hill to my right and the reviewing stand a few feet above my head, I got to the part that goes *"look away, look away, look away, Dixieland!"* Just at that moment, I saw the twirling majorettes short skirts fly up in front of me, thighs now pink from the December cold air. At some primitive snake-brain level, images of Pearl and the words of Leon and Roosevelt began mingling in my head with those of Reverend Morgan. I could see Pearl and Louise bending low and hear Roosevelt's erotic descriptions. Prurient thoughts have no sense of timing in a 16-year-old boy.

With all that going on -- and me still trying to play trombone -- a squadron of B17 bombers flew low and loud straight up Dexter Avenue, right toward the capital and that gold Jefferson Davis star. The noise drowned out my trombone, as well as the tubas, the drums and all the rest. For a moment, the band slowed and turned to watch the bombers come in so low that we could see the tail gunners and the pilots in the noses waving down at the crowd. It was just like the aviators in all the war movies I'd seen. For a moment, I so wished I were up there looking down, not over Dexter Avenue but over Berlin or Tokyo before they were bombed flat.

By this time, my heart was about to burst from all the emotion this day had kindled. The crowds, the bands, the reviewing stand, the cold air, that gold star, the B17 flyover and, last but certainly not least, the majorettes all converged to create a memory etched forever in the mind of my 16-year-old self. For all the build-up there was to this event, not one aspect of it had disappointed. Even now, 66 years later, I look back on it as one of the best days ever.

Epilogue

MAY 1, 2014

It has been 67 years since that triumphant march up Dexter Avenue in 1947 and 13 years since John's funeral in January, 2001. I will soon be 83 years old.

Once again, I stand at the foot of John's grave in the cemetery in Greenville. I stopped here on my drive down to Mobile to visit Charles. I have finished the manuscript that holds my best memories of growing up in this small town and, like reviewing one final draft of a book, I felt compelled to make this one last visit here. The memories still flood in, filled with emotions. Not grief, but a poignant sadness as I look around the cemetery at the grave markers. I no longer know a living soul in Greenville, but their bodies are still here. Of all the people I knew in town, Charles and I are the only ones still alive. I have never felt so alone or so transient.

As I walk around the cemetery I begin to see, one after another, the names of the people I knew. I pass the graves of my father and mother, as well as brother Dan and his wife Jan whose bodies were moved back to Greenville for burial. All around the cemetery, camellia bushes, now nearly tree size, are bursting with pale pink, pure white and scarlet red blooms. At one time I knew the names of each variety – Pink Perfection, Professor Sargent, Alba Plana and the Pride of Greenville. Now, I recall only a few.

I leave the cemetery to drive around town. The old business district is empty and dead. Most of the stores on Commerce Street are closed, their windows and doors boarded up. Interstate 65 now runs north of town and, like so many small towns, that's where most of the businesses have moved. The only buildings still alive on Commerce Street are the post office, City Hall, the courthouse and the Ritz Theater. A few lawyers still hang their shingles out near the courthouse. The Presbyterian, Methodist and Baptist churches still stand, but the Waller Hotel has been torn down, along with Planters' Mercantile, Beeland's General Store and the two cotton gins. The three gas stations I knew (Gulf, Shell and Sinclair) are now empty lots. I feel like I'm trapped in an old *Twilight Zone* episode where overnight a town becomes an empty shell, devoid of all signs of familiar life.

After my visit with Charles, I head back toward Nashville. Along the way, thoughts of Greenville past and present fill my head. I'm struck not only by how much it has changed, but also how much growing up there changed me. It's funny to think that my family was considered outsiders for a time back in those days because we weren't native to the town. But I think being on the outside looking in made me a keen observer of people and of life. It made me inquisitive, too. These sensibilities have served me well as a physician and now as a writer.

I began writing about Greenville and its characters 20 years ago. From time to time, I would take out the manuscript, read it over and add one or two more stories. I'm not sure I knew I was writing a book until recently, when the stories began to come

May 1, 2014

together as a picture of life in another time. I knew then I had to finish it.

This has been a labor of love. I only hope you had as much fun reading these stories as I did writing them.

About the Author

C lifton K. Meador graduated from Vanderbilt University School of Medicine in 1955, sharing the Founders' Medal for top scholastic honors with a classmate. He spent his internship and first year of residency in medicine under Dr. Robert F. Loeb at Columbia Presbyterian Hospital in New York. After two years in the U.S. Army medical corps as a Captain, he returned to Vanderbilt to complete his residency in medicine under Dr. David Rogers and to complete an N.I.H. fellowship in endocrinology under Dr. Grant Liddle. He returned to his native state and practiced medicine in Selma, Alabama, with the physician who in 1931 delivered him into life.

Dr. Tinsley Harrison, then outgoing chairman of medicine at the University of Alabama in Birmingham, recruited him to the faculty. Dr. Meador directed the N.I.H. Clinical Research Center at the university for six years, advanced to professor of medicine and served as dean of the School of Medicine at the University of Alabama in Birmingham from 1968 to 1973.

In 1973 Dr. Meador returned to Vanderbilt to join the full-time faculty as professor of medicine and to establish the Vanderbilt teaching service in medicine at Saint Thomas Hospital. Dr. Meador also served as chief medical officer of the hospital until 1998, when he became the executive director of the newly

Clifton K. Meador M.D.

formed Meharry-Vanderbilt Alliance. Retiring in 2012, he now is professor of medicine emeritus at Vanderbilt School of Medicine, enjoying writing full time.

Dr. Meador has published extensively in the medical literature; he is perhaps best known for **The Art and Science of Nondisease** and **The Last Well Person**, both published in the *New England Journal of Medicine*, and **A Lament for Invalids**, published in the *Journal of the American Medical Association*. He authored a satiric article **Clinical man: homo clinicus** in which he predicts a new species of man totally dependent on medical care, published in *Pharos*. All of the articles are satiric treatments of the excesses of medical practice. He is the author of thirteen books, including the best-selling medical books, **A Little Book of Doctors' Rules, Med School, Symptoms of Unknown Origin, Puzzling Symptoms**, and **True Medical Detective Stories**. His last book (**Fascinomas –fascinating medical mysteries**) by CreateSpace was number one in doctor-patient Kindle sales for several months.

Sketches of a Small Town… circa 1940 is his 14ᵗʰ book. These stories from childhood tell of life in a small town in the deeply segregated South during the Great Depression and World War II.

Meador lives in Nashville with his wife Ann. He is the father of seven children, seven grandchildren, and one great-granddaughter

All content © Clifton K. Meador

27182674R00106

Made in the USA
San Bernardino, CA
10 December 2015